Breaking The Yoke Of Financial Hardship
Financial Breakthrough **Secrets & Prayers**

Breaking The Yoke Of Financial Hardship
Copyright © 2018 by Olatunde Oluwabunmi Judah

ISBN: ISBN-13: 978-1539945277
ISBN-10: 1539945278

Printed by CreateSpace, An Amazon.com Company

All correspondence to:
Olatunde Oluwabunmi Judah
Divine Storm Assembly Ministries
20, Oluwole Olaniyan Street,
Iyana Ipaja.
Lagos Nigeria
Mobile: 2348067719589, E-mail: dsachurch@gmail.com

Published by: Goshen Publishing House, Lagos, Nigeria.
And Divine Storm Assembly publication
Mobile: +234 806 771 9589

Available at Amazon.com, other online stores and book stores.

Table of Content

Section Two
Financial Breakthrough Secrets

1. Breaking Out Of Poverty Cycle — 11 - 20
2. Causes of Poverty — 21 - 31
3. Understanding the need for money — 32 - 42
4. Why God wants you to be rich — 43 - 47
5. Covenant keys to financial Breakthrough — 48 - 51

Summary — **52 - 54**

Section Two
Financial Breakthrough Prayers

6. Oh Lord, Have Mercy On Me — 56 - 59
7. Oh, Lord Endue Me With Power — 60 - 63
8. Pulling Down Your Foundation Of Poverty — 64 - 67
9. Destroying The Altar of Poverty — 68 - 70
10. Breaking Ancestral Curse Of Poverty — 71 - 75
11. Arresting The Spirit of Lack and Poverty — 76 - 79
12. Breaking The Yoke Of Indebtedness — 80 - 83
13. Victory over The Enemy of Your Progress — 84 - 88
14. Breaking The Chains Of Poverty — 89 - 92
15. Stopping The Operation Of Devourers — 93 - 97
16. Silencing The Accusers Of Your Prosperity — 98 -102
17. Destroying The Operation Of Evil Hands — 103-106
18. Breaking The Network Of Darkness — 107-110
19. Commanding Anointing for Financial Favor — 111-115
20. Possessing the Power to Renewing Your Mind — 116-118
21. Heavens Of My Financial Fortune, Open — 119-123
22. Open My Eyes To My Source Of Prosperity — 124-126
23. Divine Connection To Prosperity Helpers — 127-129

24. Mantle Of Prosperity, Fall On Me   130-133

25. Prayers For Ideas For Streams Of Income   134-136

26. Breaking The Yoke Of Repeated Failure   137-141

27. My Financial Glory, Manifest   142-144

28. Breaking Out Of The Prison Of Poverty   145-149

29. Aborting Attacks Against Your
Source Of Income   150-153

30. Sending Back The Arrows Of Poverty   154-157

31. Deliverance From Spirit Spouse   158-162

32. Overcoming the Spirit of Laziness   163-166

33. Releasing Your Prosperity In Captivity   167-169

34. Victory Over Dream Criminals   170-173

35. Breaking The Yoke of Financial Hardship   174-176

36. Setting The Garment Of Poverty Ablaze   177-179

37. Beheading The Serpent Of Poverty   180-183

38. Breaking Down Every Evil Wall Of Resistance   184-186

39. Commanding The Atmosphere of Prosperity   187-190

40. Breaking the curse of slavery   191-193

41. Breaking Free From Witchcraft Operation   194-197

42. Overcoming difficulties and hardship   198-200

43. Wind of money, blow into my life   201-204

44. Conclusion   205

Dedication

I dedicate this book to the Holy Spirit, the custodian of every good and fruitful inspiration, and to those who want to leave the corridor of poverty to the arena of prosperity.

INTRODUCTION

Financial breakthrough answers to many principles one of which is prayer. Prayer has a way of making things fall into place. It redefines your life and repositions it for financial flow to come in.

Many people struggle financially, though they have great ideas, great vision, great dreams and great business. Many company and business owners are in great financial debt. People only see the branded name, products and services, yet the company is in massive debt.

If there is a business to do, there should be money to do it. If there is a flow of idea there should be money available to execute it. If there is a good job you should not be in debt. Why many people run business in debts for years is because they have not broken the jinx of financial hardship in their life and business. If you start your business with loan and you are still running it with loan now and then you need to wake up and break the jinx. Though, you may start with loan, the business should yield profit that will pay off the loan and also be enough to keep funding the business. If you start with your own capital, you should not be running it in debt or in loan, because the business should grow to a point of financially sustainability.

Business and ideas are one of the money magnets that pull in money automatically through good customer services, quality and standard products, and creative awareness and marketing. All this should make the money flow. However, if it does not, you may need to consider divine intervention by prayer.

Money is the running fuel of business. The way it will take gas to keep a vehicle engine in motion, so it will take money to keep a business running. Staff has to be paid, raw materials has to be purchased, and adverts has to be done, all with money. Money makes the business run a complete circle of profit. Learn to put more emphasis on making money in that business so that you don't run it on loan.

Prayer is ordained to create the world of possibilities, to dig out the things of the spirit and make them the babes of the physical. Prayer is the force that creates; faith is the force that delivers. Prayer brings to manifestation what has been lying dormant in the spiritual realm. Through the force of prayer, hidden things are been revealed, and solution is been given to resolve a matter.

How to get the best of this book

Every book give you a chance to change something about your life, this book give you a chance to change everything about your financial life. What you need to get into financial prosperity is

1. **Follow the instructions:**
    Take fast hold of instruction; let [her] not go: keep her; for she [is] thy life. Prov. 4:13

    Instruction delivers from destruction. Instructions are guidelines that usher you into the path of success. Divine instruction will bring you into your breakthrough.

2. **Embark on 21days or 40days fasting with the prayers:**
    [Is] not this the fast that I have chosen? *to loose the bands of wickedness, to undo the heavy burdens, and to let the oppressed go free, and*

that ye break every yoke? [Is it] not to deal thy bread to the hungry, and that thou bring the poor H6041 that are cast out to thy house? when thou seest the naked, that thou cover him; and that thou hide not thyself from thine own flesh? Then shall thy light break forth as the morning, and thine health shall spring forth speedily: and thy righteousness shall go before thee; the glory of the LORD shall be thy rereward.
Then shalt thou call, and the LORD shall answer; thou shalt cry, and he shall say, Here I [am]. If thou take away from the midst of thee the yoke, the putting forth of the finger, and speaking vanity; Isa 58:6-9

Fasting means staying away from food and water for some hours in a day or days depending on the kind of fasting you embark on. You can stay without water from morning to evening by 6pm while you embark on fervent prayers. You break in the evening. You are not starving yourself for fun, but you are engaging spiritual keys to breaking yokes and bondages holding you bound to that force.

Insight on fasting

Daily fast:
You will not each food or drink water till evening by 6pm, after you can eat and drink water. *So we fasted and besought our God for this: and he was intreated of us. Ezra 8:23*

Dry fast:
Being forty days tempted of the devil. And in those days he did eat nothing: and when they were ended, he afterward hungered. Luke 4:2
You don't eat or drink water for minimum of 3days. It depends on how many days you body has the capacity to carry you. It may be 3days, 5days, 7days or more.

3. **Pray day and night:**
Evening , and morning, and at noon, will I pray, and cry aloud: and he shall hear my voice. Ps 55:17

The effectual fervent prayer of the righteous availed much. Effective prayer is done in the spirit with fasting involved in it. Prayer is the weapon to remove untold impossibilities and create a possibility environment for smooth financial success in life and every other area of life. In this case you pray for baptism of idea that will change your life forever.

4. **Give sacrificial seed of financial turnaround:**
    Giving is living. Giving open doors to opportunities and divine blessing. Giving is a spiritual principle that makes way for you to receive. Be not deceived whatever a man sows, he shall reap. Giving brings harvest. It must be clear and not neglected.

Section One
Financial Breakthrough Secrets

1
Breaking Out Of Poverty Cycle

The rich man's wealth [is] his strong city: the destruction of the poor [is] their poverty. Prov. 10:15

Poverty is a destiny destroyer. People with great destinies have been trapped under the spell of poverty. Poverty has become the life companion of many gifted people. Poverty is like an infection that doesn't cure on its own until it is treated with right medications. However, poverty does not stop anyone from making it, except those who chose to remain in it. It should not be given a chance to thrive beyond *now* in your life.

The truth is that you may be born poor but you are not permitted to remain poor. Poverty is not your portion in Christ that is why it has to be eradicated in your life. Poverty does not profit anyone. It is a man without a dream that will desire to be poor. Poverty is a reproach and does not glorify God.

Everyone wants to get out of the rat race, but many are confused as to how to do it, you have the key here. The truth is that poverty has a force behind it. The force of poverty is a force that keeps one generation to another in poverty. Poverty is a negative force that ravages his victims and keeps them under its stronghold.

Poverty is a wicked force that steals the dream of her victim and makes her victim amount to less than his dream. When poverty put on his victim like a garment it will glue on them so much that it will take a determined man to remove it with every available effort. Don't celebrate poverty, there is no goodnews in been poor.

To break out simply means to be free from the grip of poverty. The word break means to shatter something, to hit something so hard till it shatter into pieces, to hit something with a force so that it can give way to you. To break out means to shatter the barrier of poverty and come out into prosperity.

It does not matter how long you have been under the stronghold of poverty, Jesus has the power to deliver you. Jesus is the head of every principality and power. Nothing is too hard for him to do. Poverty will not be your ruin in Jesus name. Those in the prison of poverty need to be free so that they can thirst the beauty of life in the land of the living.

For the LORD hath redeemed Jacob, and ransomed him from the hand of [him that was] stronger than he. Jer 31:11

If the force of poverty is too strong for you to break out of, it is not too strong for God. God has the power to ransom you from the power of generational poverty. Poverty is a dream killer, a destiny destroyer, a silencer. It silences talents, skills, ideas and dreams.

God's delight is to see you free from this shameful enemy. There is nothing that can stop God and there is nothing that will stop you in Jesus name.

Four Categories Of People

At the end of your life you will fall into one of these categories. You have a choice to decide which category you belong.

1. **Born rich and die poor**

    Many are born into a wealthy family only to die wretched. However, you have a choice of how you want to end. If you were born into a rich home, learn the secret of their prosperity, if it is genuine then put it to practice and maintain the status of the family you were born into so that you can pass that riches to the next generation as well.

2. **Born poor and die rich**

    These sets of people are the ones who were born into a poor family, they experienced poverty, but they cannot afford to remain in poverty and out of their passion to breakout out, they succeeded and became rich and died rich. Breaking out of the cycle of abject poverty is one of the greatest fights you need to undertake. If some people can break out, you can break out too. You can only break out of poverty if you have zero tolerance for it. If you are comfortable you may remain in it, don't be comfortable.

    What you don't passionately desire to be you can't become by chance except it has being preordained for you. God is ready to deliver you from poverty and prosper you with the blessing of Abraham in Christ Jesus.

3. **Born rich and die rich**

These set of people are wise enough to maintain their status. They were born rich and they sustain their wealth through wisdom, humility and grace. These are one of the hardest and also simplest status to maintain throughout life time. The ability to maintain an inherited wealth is a great task. So if you are born rich, do everything possible to maintain the status. Don't be frugal; also endeavour to have financial advisers before making a major financial decision.

If for one reason or the other you don't value your inheritance of a rich family background there is a possibility of losing it cheaply. You must appreciate wealth enough to sustain it, but don't worship it as your god.

4. **Born poor and die poor**
   These are the set of people who helplessly found themselves in the cycle of poverty and actually remain trapped in it for life. Under this category, there are two sets of people. First set are those who were born poor, but they had opportunity that brought in riches at one time or the other but mismanaged it and went back poor, for example are those who have won jackpot, lotto, even some financial breakthrough, soccer and music stars, etc.

   Then the second set, are those who were actually born poor and were never privileged to thirst wealth all their life till they died. That is poverty from birth to burial. These are people under chronic force of inherited poverty. These categories of people never knew what it takes to enjoy riches, though it is not a sin to die poor, but it is not the will of God to die poor.

A good [man] leaveth an inheritance to his children's children: and the wealth of the sinner [is] laid up for the just. Prov. 13:22

These categories only lived their life as spectator and a witness. They wondered how people become rich and they watched the rich enjoy their riches. And some even served the rich. Nonetheless to some of them life is still beautiful that way.

You must make every possible effort in the right direction to break-out of the cycle of poverty you find yourself. Draw close to God and break every curse and pull down every stronghold of poverty, be careful how you live your life and don't allow negative influence of wrong association to waste your opportunities.

You can make it to the rich list if you passionately desire it. Desire is the evidence of want. Thou, desire is not enough, learning the keys to moving from poverty to prosperity is needed as well. One of such key is prayer. Why prayer is needed is to clear every physical and satanic obstacle that can stop you from attaining your dream. Prosperity is the will of God for you and not poverty.

Prayer engineers the operation of heavenly forces to work in your favour and bring your dreams and visions to reality. It is written that surely there is an end, your expectation will not cut off. It is through prayer that your expectations are granted. Praying is evidence of desire to get out of the circle of poverty and your desire will push you to go all the way to make it happen.

Types Of Poverty

1. **Financial and material poverty:**
   This is a state of physical lack and not having enough to meet up with your daily lives need. It is having less than you should, not having enough of money and enough of substance, but only sustained daily by the little that comes in from your day to day activities.

2. **Intellectual poverty:**
   It is a state of lacking skills, idea, talent, gifts that can attract wealth and riches into your life. There are people who are clueless. They have no skill, have not discovered their talent or gift or don't know how to put it to use.

3. **Mental poverty:**
   It is a poor state of mind. A poor mind will produce a poor man. It is a state of desiring less, lacking dreams and passion to succeed. Mental poverty makes people in this category to believe some people are born to be rich why some others are just created to be poor. People suffering from mental poverty hate the rich and even see wealth as a taboo. They have to be delivered from this kind of wrong mind-set.

4. **Spiritual poverty:**
   It is a state of spiritual dryness in someone. When the spiritual life of a person is totally dead and the carnal mind is completely alive, where the man in question has no

desire for the things of the spirit. Spiritual poverty arise from carnality. It is a state of being totally carnal (walking and living in the flesh all day) minded and spiritually lost. People in this category don't have significance for spiritual principles that can turn around their spiritual status and financial fortune.

However, spiritual poverty can be eradicated by desiring to grow in the things of the Spirit and getting close to God through his word and his service.

5. **Character poverty:**

It is a situation where someone lacks manners and character. A good character is an asset. It adds value to yourself worth, it open doors to you where it matters and bring opportunities your way. Symptoms of character deficiency is being saucy, proud, full of dirty words, lack ethics, do things without reasoning, fighting, snubbing people, making jest of people, bullying people instead of loving them, causing problems and so forth. Everyone has the personal responsibility to work on their character for the betterment of their person.

A quality character give you influence and get you connected to right people. A quality character is the trademark of a quality lifestyle. Quality characters reflect the rich values you possess as individual. A rich character is a mark of integrity; it is what you are and not what you want to be. You have to work on yourself. If you don't deal with your poverty, your poverty will deal with you. Deal with it now.

Keys To Breaking Out Of The Prison Of Poverty

1. **Give your life to Jesus:**
Why you need to give your life to Jesus.

For ye know the grace of our Lord Jesus Christ, that, though he was rich, yet for your sakes he became poor, that ye through his poverty might be rich. 2Cor 8:9

There is an inheritance Jesus has secured for you. If you were born poor and you have given your life to Christ, you are no more poor. He has purchased riches for you through his blood. Just give your life to Him and all that will be yours.

And for those who already has the riches, there is something more than riches in Christ, it is called eternal life. Eternal life makes you identify with Jesus and with God. Without eternal life you are not save and you cannot be safe from judgment and torment of the devil, but Jesus says.

And I give unto them eternal life; and they shall never perish, neither shall any [man] pluck them out of my hand. John 10:28

Receive eternal life in Jesus and your life will be safe from fear and terror.

2. **Discover the causes behind your poverty:**
Discovery brings recovery. When you discover the sources of your problem, the problem is half solved. When you

make effort in the right direction, the problem will be totally solved. Discover the source, you can read how in Chapter two.

3. **Engage violent prayer and fasting:**
   If any force of darkness has been responsible for your poverty, through the force of prayer and fasting there yoke will be broken. Fasting and prayer are twins, they go hand in hand. You can't fast without praying. Fasting is a key to breaking satanic yoke and removing obstacles.

   [Is] not this the fast that I have chosen? to loose the bands of wickedness, to undo the heavy burdens, and to let the oppressed go free, and that ye break every yoke? Isa 58:6

   Fasting and prayer is a combination of spiritual armour that is too powerful for burdens and stronghold of poverty in your life to withstand. It delivers per time.

4. **Deploy relevant spiritual weapons to destroy the stronghold of poverty:**
   (For the weapons of our warfare [are] not carnal, but mighty through God to the pulling down of strong holds;) 2Cor 10:4.
   Spiritual weapons are needed to fight invisible battles. The word of God is a powerful weapon. It is called the sword of the spirit in *Ephesians 6:17*, it is called fire and hammer in Jer. 23:29, it is called God in John 1:1. The word of God is an irresistible weapon of warfare. Other weapons are prayer Luke 18:1-9, the name of Jesus phil.2:9-11, the anointing oil Isaiah 10:27, the blood of Jesus Zech. 9:11, seed (i.e financial or material offering) Luke 8:36. Deploy

every spiritual weapon in your custody to fight every battle till you overcome them.

5. **Acquire relevant knowledge and information:**
Knowledge is power. Knowledge is a force of change. The more you know the better you become. Knowledge is helpful, it takes you out of the valley and place you upon the hill for the world to see. If you have a gift in you, you need adequate knowledge to sharpen the gift and sell the gift. There is something also so special about knowledge,

Through wisdom is an house builded; and by understanding it is established: And by knowledge shall the chambers be filled with all precious and pleasant riches. Prov. 24:3-4.

It takes wisdom to build an empire; it takes knowledge to acquire riches for the empire. A man that lacks knowledge will end in shame. You need knowledge of making money, knowledge of selling your gift, talents, idea etc. knowledge makes navigation easy. When you know a city, you can drive all around the city in a jivy, but when you don't know, you will end where you started without driving to a destination. Adequate knowledge of your trade(what you are doing) is needed to fill your bank account with money.

2
Causes of Poverty

How long wilt thou sleep, O sluggard? When wilt thou arise out of thy sleep? [Yet] a little sleep, a little slumber, a little folding of the hands to sleep: So shall thy poverty come as one that travelleth, and thy want as an armed man.
Prov. 6:9-11

People are not poor on purpose. Poverty has a source and when the source of a problem is discovered, it is easy to sort a solution for it but if it is not discovered the people will remain perpetually in it bondage. Poverty can either be inherited or can be as a result of one of these factors.

1. **Disobedience to God's word:**
    If they obey and serve him, they shall spend their days in prosperity, and their years in pleasures. But if they obey not, they shall perish by the sword, and they shall die without knowledge. Job 36:11-12 (NIV).
    Many people are under the spell of poverty because they have violated God's word. The devil always looks for a legal ground to keep his victim in bondage. One of the good legal grounds he uses for his victim is disobedience to God's word. God's word contains the principle for prosperity.

2. **Lack of knowledge:**
    My people are destroyed for lack of knowledge: because thou hast rejected knowledge, I will also reject thee, that thou shalt be no priest to me: seeing thou hast forgotten the law of thy God, I will also forget thy children. Hosea 4:6

Lack of knowledge keeps people in the bondage of ignorance. Knowledge means to know something that will help you to become what you want to be, and to know what Christ has put in place to make your life colorful. A man without knowledge will feel inferior to a man who has it and he will end up being a servant to the latter.

3. **Lack of education:**
Formal education plays a factor in acquiring relevant educative knowledge to break out of poverty to prosperity. Illiteracy is the enemy of success. Stack illiterate have the tendency to suffer stack poverty. Education will give you a platform to showcase what you got to the world. Any village or community where the people are not educated will ravage in abject poverty. Lack of education does not make everyone poor, but major underdeveloped communities and villages as a result of poverty is lack of formal and informal education of her people.

There are two kind of education
There is *formal education* and there is an *informal education*. Formal education is going to school at the lowest level to the level of obtaining a degree on what you have applied to become. Some people just need the former education to climb the ladder of success, why everyone needs the informal education. Informal education is acquiring relevant knowledge, information and skills that will launch you out of the valley of the masses to the peak of greatness.

4. **Lack of idea:**

Idea is what some people need to change their financial status and so when they lack the right idea, they will lack the opportunity of ever becoming financially free. Idea they say rule the world.

Idea is a divine inspiration that is received to bless humanity. Idea is conceiving a powerful inspiration on what to do to be a blessing to mankind and receive financial reward back in return. Every great idea that is well maximized will change the financial fortune of the owner.

There is a life changing idea and there is a eyes opening idea that is non-profitable. You must be able to get down with the idea that will change people's life and change your status.

5. Lack of vision:

Where [there is] no vision, the people perish: but he that keepeth the law, happy [is] he. Prov.29:18.

When you see a drop out that ended up becoming a multi-millionaire, it's because he has a vision greater than the formal education. When people lack vision, there will not be a drive to achieve anything worthwhile. Lack of vision is lack of motivation. It makes the subject lack motivation for success. Vision is a powerful factor that drives in prosperity.

6. Lack of divine direction:

Divine direction is powerful key of connecting to your divine opportunities. Divine direction is when God lead you to your source of opportunities that will launch you into your prosperity. Everyone needs to be led by God into his place of fortune. Without divine direction and leading good effort can end in vain.

7. **Lack of destiny helpers:**

Many people never succeed because they lack helpers. Helpers are those people God brought your way to give you a platform to make it financially. There are two kinds of helpers, God as your helper and God using men as an agent of help for you. When a person lacks human help, it is because he lacks divine help. The first kind of help a man needs is divine help. Divine help will open door to human help. When God is ready to change a man situation, He will send someone is way who will show him compassion and assist him to carry his burden.

8. **Lack of divine favor:**

Favor is a divine virtue that is released by God upon a man to attract substance. Favor is an aura of blessing upon a person. Lack of favor is the lack of aura to attract good things into one's life. Favor is a covering that will remove shame and reproach of poverty from a man's life. Favor makes your work prosper in your hands. A person that carries favor will attract easy financial flow in what they do. Thou, favor is in levels. There is a general favor, the favor enjoyed by most people, and there is a royal favor. The favor experienced by only very few people. You can move to the next level of favor with good deed and mercy of God.

9. **Lack of financial intelligence skill:**

Lack of financial intelligence skills means not knowing how to channel your money into profitable ventures. Some people make money at one time or the other, but lost it as a result of inadequate financial planning and management. Go and learn how to spend, how to save, how to invest and where to invest.

10. Laziness:

He becometh poor that dealeth [with] a slack hand: but the hand of the diligent maketh rich. Prov. 10:4

Laziness is the state of not wanting to do anything. Just want things to happen on their own without making any effort. Laziness is when you have offers, opportunities, even jobs but you abandon them to play or to sleep. A lazy man is born to suffer. Laziness is one of the strongholds of poverty. Don't give room for laziness.

11. Lack of divine instruction:

Poverty and shame [shall be to] him that refuseth instruction: but he that regardeth reproof shall be honoured. Prov. 13:18

Divine instruction is the step by step guide on how to do wants you must do to get the result you must get. There is divine instruction for every man. Every product has an instruction manual on how it will be operated for best performance. Divine Instruction delivers from destruction and bring you divine elevation. Some people's success in life is attached to divine instruction, without receiving the instruction they will remain in one spot without been able to change the situation.

12. Lack of opportunities:

Some people lack opportunities. They are not in an advantage location to tap into an opportunity that will change their lives. As a matter of fact, opportunity is one of the major key to financial breakthrough. A man needs to come in contact with major opportunities in life and his financial status will change. Sometimes it happens as a result of not taking cognizance of information that would have been a blessing to you.

13. Procrastination:

Procrastinator is someone who defers what he ought to do now till another day. Procrastinators are time waster and opportunity killer. They waste opportunities that will change their lives and let it slip away. Procrastinators are less committed to what can make their life better. Procrastinators cannot enjoy recommendation of the nobles.

14. Wrong investment:

Investment is a vehicle of multiplying your money. Investment is not savings but rather keeping your money into a profitable venture to make good returns. Nevertheless, if you make bad investment decision and the money end up without returns that will amount to a major shortage or lose. Many people have lost what they have acquired over the years to wrong investment and they have come to nothing. You must be careful before you commit your money to any investment. The wrong investment can bring a rich man down to nothing.

15. Wrong association:

He that walketh with wise [men] shall be wise: but a companion of fools shall be destroyed. Prov. 13:20

There is a saying that says, show me your friend and I will tell you who you are. The people you move with determine the fruit you produce. The aura of your companion will rob on you. You have the tendency to be influenced by those you move with on a daily basis. If you work with fools, the end result will be gory because fools have no delight in wisdom.

You association determines your motivation, and your motivation determines your elevation. You can hardly go farther than your cycle of company.

16. Ancestral curse and evil covenants:

Curse is a negative utterance issued upon a person or family as a result of wrong deed of the individual or family in order to suffer the consequence of their evil deed. Some people are suffering from curse of poverty, to suffer for the wickedness of their ancestors or they themselves. Ancestral curse is an inherited curse that moves from one generation to the other. Generational curse comes as a result of the wickedness, sins, disobedience of their ancestors.

Evil covenant can also be responsible for the poverty of some people. For those whose ancestors has entered into certain covenant with an idol, a deity or certain personality that is required to be observed from one generation to the other but now has been neglected, the covenant will begin to fight against the destiny of those under it uniformly. The curse they inherited from their foundation and the evil covenant working in their foundation will work together to keep them in bondage until it is broken they cannot be free.

17. Inherited evil foundation:

If the foundations be destroyed, what can the righteous do? Ps 11:3
The right foundation will produce the right fruit while the wrong foundation will produce a corrupt fruit. You are a product of your foundation any day and any time. Your foundation is your beginning, your origin, your root, your bloodline and all that patterns to your make up physically and spiritually. If your foundation has inheritance of poverty and you don't break out of such foundation, such person will live in poverty.

18. Repeated evil attacks:

Demonic attacks against people's destiny can stop the flow of good things and abortion of expectation. If a person operates under satanic oppression he cannot make good financial decision and money cannot flow into his life until the stronghold of darkness is shattered.

19. Lack of motivation:

Motivation is the desire to succeed. Lack of motivation means there is nothing driving you to prosper. When there is no motivation there will be no upward and forward movement. Motivation is driven by a dream, a goal, a desire and a passion. Without the motivation needed, the inspiration to create ideas and strategies that will turn your desire for prosperity into reality will be lacking. Motivation brings determination to succeed.

20. **Addiction to destructive habits:**
Addiction to wrong habit will bring wreckage to destiny. Addiction like betting and taking drugs can cause poverty. That habit will make you to gather and also waste your hard earned money on it.

21. **Love of pleasure:**
He that loveth pleasure [shall be] a poor man: he that loveth wine and oil shall not be rich. Prov 21:17
This category of people spends their lives in clubs, in bars, drinking, wining and dining with harlots. And never have any left over. They make money to waste the money on frugal living.

22. **Joblessness:**
A jobless man will suffer lack. Joblessness is not the same as laziness. Jobless means you have no job and no work you are doing. You must do something if you want money. Money does not flow into the bosom of the man that has nothing doing. However, some people are not lazy but they feel too big to work under anyone, and yet they have no money or idea to start any establishment in that case they remain humbled by poverty.

23. **Wrong attitude to money:**
Those with wrong attitude and mind-set towards riches and prosperity can hardly make it. Some people see making money as a taboo and others believed wealth can only be gotten through crooked means.

Two [things] have I required of thee; deny me [them] not before I die:
Remove far from me vanity and lies: give me neither poverty nor
riches; feed me with food convenient for me:
Lest I be full, and deny [thee], and say, Who [is] the LORD? or
lest I be poor, and steal, and take the name of my God [in vain].
Prov 30:7-9.

Your attitude and mind-set will affect your access to prosperity. You must develop the right attitude for money if you want money. Believing that money belongs to some set people alone is a wrong mind-set for money. Money belongs to no one.

24. Habit of Wasting resources

He also that is slothful in his work is brother to him that is a great waster.
Prov. 18:9

People with this kind of habits are called wasters. Wasters are the people that waste resources, waste opportunities, waste supplies. Wasters will exhaust the resources that could have been reserved and used in a better way. A waster never see reason why he should preserve left over, he never see reason to save, he never reason to gather for increase. He blows all he has at once.

Go to the ant, thou sluggard; consider her ways, and be wise: Which
having no guide, overseer, or ruler, Provideth her meat in the summer,
[and] gathereth her food in the harvest. Prov 6:6-8.

The word of God says you can learn from the ant. The ant has no guide, no overseer (supervisor) but yet knows how to gather little and turn it to plenty. Learn from it. It is little but considered as wise. Wisdom is learning how to save, manage and gather for increase.

25. Spell and bad luck:

Spell and bad luck spirit in a man's life will bring him to abject poverty. Spell is the spirit of blunder making people to make costly mistake at crucial moment of a turning point. And when a spell is at work in a man's life, he will be experiencing constant bad luck. The Jinx of spell and bad luck can be broken through an effectual fervent prayer.

3
Understanding The Need For Money

A feast is made for laughter, and wine maketh merry: but money answereth all [things]. Eccl 10:19

Money answers all things. Money is so important that no one can live throughout life without having a need for it. Money is one of the most needed resources on earth. Every home needs money, every person needs money, the government needs money, our need for money will never end. Money is part of our everyday pursuit because of the purpose it serves. When you stop making money, there is a tendency you will stop making progress.

Money is very important in executing projects, visions and plans. If there is no money per time, purpose may be disappointed. Money contributes largely to every small and great achievement of men. Money is a vital force of life. Money is part of the substance you need to acquire to make life comfortable and pleasurable. Every part of life requires money. You need money to be educated, to take care of your family, to meet your needs, to support others.

You need money to survive. People wake up early because of money, go to bed late because of money and have sleepless night because of money. Yet, only to wake up and think of how to make money and money seems difficult to come. Anyone who crash into money by accident, will have money leave him by accident. Money thrives in the hand of the wise. *Money comes to the hand of the labourer, it increases in the hand of an investor, and vanish in the hand of a spender.*

What the Scriptures Says About Money

But money answereth all things

A feast is made for laughter, and wine maketh merry: but money answereth all [things]. Eccl 10:19

Every activities of men involves money. Without money many dreams will remain in the incubation plant and will never see the light of the day. Many people have died without achieving their dreams and vision. It was kept in there diary, vision book, in their memory card, brain box or their wardrobe and could not be given birth to because there was no money.

Every dreams, vision and venture runs on money. The gospel of the Lord Jesus requires money to spread. God knows the importance of money in the spreading of the gospel.

Cry yet, saying, Thus saith the LORD of hosts; My cities through prosperity shall yet be spread abroad; and the LORD shall yet comfort Zion, and shall yet choose Jerusalem. Zech 1:17

It takes prosperity to spread the gospel. It takes prosperity to enlarge and expand on every side. In everything money is needed.

Money is a defence

For wisdom [is] a defence, [and] money [is] a defence: but the excellency of knowledge [is, that] wisdom giveth life to them that have it. Eccl 7:12

Money keeps one from shame and reproach. No matter the level of your spirituality, you can't live without spending money. Everything around you is sustained by God and then money. You must pay the rent of the house you live, you must pay for the food stuff, gas, children school fees and other things. You need money to meet all this demands. You cannot deny you need for money. Without money you are defenseless, often times when you have an important bill to pay and you lack money, all you can do is to seek for permission to pay at a later date. If you cannot afford to pay your rent, your stuff may be locked outside the property you occupy. So money is a defence. When you have it, it will defend you from assault of your landlord, and also from shame and reproach among peers and family.

Money belongs to God

The silver [is] mine, and the gold [is] mine, saith the LORD of hosts. Hag 2:8

Silver and gold here refers to money. God owns money and not the devil. Anyone that seeks the devil for money will suffer great loss at the end. Devil gives nothing for free. Devil gives people money at the cost of their life and blood, God gives money at the price of grace and mercy. That is why it is the blessing of God that makes one rich and adds no sorrow according to proverbs 10:22. The blessing of the devil adds lots of sorrow and unrest.

Money should be invested

Then you should have deposited my money with the bankers, and on my return I would have received my money back with interest! Matt 25:27. (Net Bible).

Jesus said in the parable of the talent, that the money given to the third man, atleast should be invested so that it can bring forth more money. Not all money should be consumed. Money can increase through the right investment.

In his book breaking financial hardship, Bishop Oyedepo wrote:
When you do the right thing with your ten naira, it will become one hundred naira. When you do the right thing with your one hundred naira, it will become one thousand naira, and when you do the right thing with your one thousand naira, it will become ten thousand naira, and when you do the right thing with your one thousand naira, it will become one hundred thousand naira. By the time you do the right thing with your one hundred thousand naira, it will become one million naira. Do the right thing with one million naira, and it is on it way to becoming one billion naira!. That is the way it works.

Money has the capacity to multiply itself if it is well planned and invested. Single money invested in the right thing can turn to double, and double money invested rightly will multiply to fourfold. You must learn the art of growing your money.

Do not love money
For the love of money is the root of all evils. Some people in reaching for it have strayed from the faith and stabbed themselves with many pains. 1Tim 6:10

There is nothing wrong in making money, but there is everything wrong in loving money. Love blindfolds people from the truth. The love of money makes people lost their integrity and become corrupt in their dealings. If the love of money has crept into your heart, you must cast it out, because when money is deeply love, men will compromise and do anything legal or illegal to make it, not looking at the consequences behind their action. Those who love money in order word idolize money and make it their god.

Money gives you a voice

After they arrived in Capernaum, the collectors of the temple tax came to Peter and said, "Your teacher pays the double drachma tax, doesn't he?" He said, "Yes." When Peter came into the house, Jesus spoke to him first, "What do you think, Simon? From whom do earthly kings collect tolls or taxes — from their sons or from foreigners?" After he said, "From foreigners," Jesus said to him, "Then the sons are free.

But so that we don't offend them, go to the lake and throw out a hook. Take the first fish that comes up, and when you open its mouth, you will find a four drachma coin. Take that and give it to them for me and you." Matt 17:24-27.

Money gives you the chance to help others. Money makes people to listen to what you have to say. Money give you command over situation and put you at advantage position to effects every good plans without delay. Money has a voice and it gives you a voice.

Who Owns Money

It is very important to know who owns money. It is the person that owns money that can give you money.

The silver [is] mine, and the gold [is] mine, saith the LORD of hosts. Hag 2:8

It is God that owns money. God owns the earth and all the resources used in making money. Everything belongs to God. If you need abundance of money to meet beyond your needs and meet the needs of others, you must first identify the owner of money.

God owns money and he can give anyone he chooses to give and also give those who desire it. If God wants to make a man rich, he gives him the power to get wealth...afterward whatever he does attract abundant of money.

And thou say in thine heart, My power and the might of [mine] hand hath gotten me this wealth. But thou shalt remember the LORD thy God: **for [it is] he that giveth thee power to get wealth,** *that he may establish his covenant which he sware unto thy fathers, as [it is] this day. Deut 8:17-18*

When God gives you the power to get wealth, anything you do will attract so much money that you will wonder where all the money is coming from. The power there is the divine ability from God to gather wealth. It doesn't come as a result of your personal effort.

How To Get God To Give You Money

- **Delight yourself in the Lord:**
  Delight thyself also in the LORD; and he shall give thee the desires of thine heart. Ps 37:4
  Then shalt thou delight thyself in the LORD; and I will cause thee to ride upon the high places of the earth, and feed thee with the heritage of Jacob thy father: for the mouth of the LORD hath spoken [it]. Isa 58:14

  When you delight yourself in the Lord, the Lord will make you His delight. God becomes your interest and focus when you delight yourself in him. When you are God's delight, there is nothing good that will miss you. God decorate those who delight in him with enviable blessing.

- **Seek the Kingdom of God:**
  But seek ye first the kingdom of God, and his righteousness; and all these things shall be added unto you. Matt 6:33.

  God's seekers are God's lovers. God lovers are God's favorite; they win the heart of God by their quest to know him. God want you to focus on him alone. When you seek God and his kingdom with a genuine heart, God will cause money to seek you without end. Seeking God is not negotiable to enjoying the blessing of God.

- **Be an addicted giver:**
  Give, and it shall be given unto you; good measure, pressed down, and shaken together, and running over, shall men give into your bosom. For with the same measure that ye mete withal it shall be measured to you again. Luke 6:38

  Giving is meeting spiritual or physical needs that will in turn give God room the opportunity to meet your material and spiritual need. Giving is the key that open the door of God's treasury. *Luke 6:38*. Giving is commanded. Giving is sowing a seed into God's work, giving those in need, giving to worthy cause that will make God happy. Giving changes your level and continuous giving will keep changing your life. Giving is a powerful key to getting more, because whatever you give is a seed, and what you will get in return is a massive harvest. You will always get more than what you give. You can give your way to financial fortune. Just be led by God in your giving.

- **Be a tither:**

You must live a life of tithing. Every money coming into your hand as your money must be tithed. Tithing is commanded.

Bring ye all the tithes into the storehouse, that there may be meat in mine house, and prove me now herewith, saith the LORD of hosts, if I will not open you the windows of heaven, and pour you out a blessing, that [there shall] not [be room] enough [to receive it]. And I will rebuke the devourer for your sakes, and he shall not destroy the fruits of your ground; neither shall your vine cast her fruit before the time in the field, saith the LORD of hosts. And all nations shall call you blessed: for ye shall be a delightsome land, saith the LORD of hosts. Mal. 3:10-12.

Tithe is a key that opens unto you the windows of heaven of divine blessing. Blessing is the empowerment to get rich. Tithe is ten percent of every money you earn or made as profit. It is a covenant key that open the windows of heaven for outpouring of God's blessing upon the tither. Tither is someone faithful in paying tithe.

- **By walking in the covenant:**
  Keep therefore the words of this covenant, and do them, that ye may prosper in all that ye do. Deut 29:9.
  The word of God is his covenant. When the word of God is put into work, God is put into motion to keep the word of His covenant.

How To Increase Money

1. **Earn money:** Money has to be earned either by working for it, or by doing business to make it. Money you don't have you can't increase. It takes having it

before investing it. If you don't have a seed you cannot plant one.

2. **Save money:** Every money that comes into your hand must not be wasted on personal needs alone. You must cultivate the habit of saving money. Money save is better than money spent.

3. **Seed money:** Money must be given to worthy cause. Every money in your hand is a seed until you give it out, you cannot see the potential it has to bring back more. Money giving is money invested, it is not money lost. Seeded money is different from spent money. Seeded money is money you sow to a good course which will in turn come back as a blessing at the time appointed.

4. **Invest money:** Investment is a way of fast multiplying money and increasing money. Money can be invested into business of your own or other business that will bring good return.

5. **Create streams of income:** streams of income are actually different investment, different channels of earning money. The more channels you open to making money the more money that flows into your life. You can create streams of incoming by setting up different businesses or opening one business in different location as it expands and as demand increases.

6. **Command money:** command means to issue word of authority to your money. You can speak to your money to work for you, to increase daily. Command what you want your money to achieve for you. Money has ears, it will obey the voice of your command. The book of *Job 38:12, Hast thou commanded the morning since thy days; [and] caused the dayspring to know his place.*

You can give command to anything created by God or man by the authority in the name of Jesus and it will obey you. You can command your money to grow wherever you invest it, you can command it to attract more money to you.

How Not To Acquire Money

- You must not steal money to have it, you will pay back in the hard way.
- You must not kill for money, you will suffer the same fate.
- You must not do drug, you will earn yourself a life of pain.
- You must not sell your soul to the devil for money, or else you will end where he ended.
- You must not dupe people, or else you will carry God's judgment and a curse.
- You must not sacrifice human being for money, blood will be crying after you and you will end badly.

The truth is that money is not a ghost, and money can be acquired in legal ways. You don't need to be dubious to make money; you can make it the right way. Just anyone can make money, but it takes God to give you riches. *The blessing of the LORD, it maketh rich, and he addeth no sorrow with it. Prov. 10:22.* Riches are money beyond what you labor for.

4
Why God Wants You To Be Rich

Let them shout for joy, and be glad, that favour my righteous cause: yea, let them say continually, Let the LORD be magnified, which hath pleasure in the prosperity of his servant. Ps 35:27

God has pleasure in your prosperity. God does not create you to suffer in the land of the living. That is why God has gone all the way to give you Jesus to deliver you from the devil that came to kill, to steal and to destroy and from the hand of poverty that can make you ask where is the God of Abraham.

God has prepared fortune as part of his inheritance for you. God wants his own people to experience the beauty of his glory. The way God cannot bear his children suffering in pain, so he cannot bear them suffering from poverty. Poverty is not a desirable state for anyone. God wants the best for you. Any unpalatable situation you are going through in the hand of poverty is not the will of God but you have to make a choice to break out of the grip of poverty.

There is no biological father that will want to see his children suffer under the agony of poverty. It is an issue of concern to see your children going through abject poverty. God does not have poverty in plans for his children. He has designed a plot to make life a memorable place for them. God is a master planner, and he has planned for your prosperity.

For I know the thoughts that I think toward you, saith the LORD, thoughts of peace, and not of evil, to give you an expected end. Jer. 29:11

God has good thought for you. The thought God has for you is simply the thought to make life a better life for you. Good thought does not involve living a life of suffering and shame. It involves a life of comfort and peace.

1. **God owns riches:**
    The silver [is] mine, and the gold [is] mine, saith the LORD of hosts. Hag 2:8.

    God owns the silver and the gold. He owns the money and all there is in the earth. Don't let anyone convince otherwise. Devil owns nothing. He only steal from the ignorant and give to his own at a price of their soul. Everything the devil gives has a question mark. Don't take from the devil, come to Jesus He is the true custodian of riches.

2. **God is your father:**
    And because ye are sons, God hath sent forth the Spirit of his Son into your hearts, crying, Abba, Father. Gal 4:6.

    God is the father of all true believers. If God is your father you are entitled to the blessing of God. Every father has an inheritance to leave for their children. As a child of God you are not exempted.

3. **God is a rewarder:**
    God rewards those who diligently seek him. *But without faith [it is] impossible to please [him]: for he that cometh to God*

must believe that he is, and [that] he is a rewarder of them that diligently seek him. Heb 11:6

God rewards those who come after in truth and spirit to serve and adore him. Seekers of God are never in want. For God is a rewarder. He rewards you with the desires of your heart and what He dims fit for his glory in your life.

4. **You are the heir of salvation:**
   And if ye [be] Christ's, then are ye Abraham's seed, and heirs according to the promise. Gal 3:29
   An heir is entitled to the throne and every benefit that accrues to the throne of his father. As heir of God, you are entitled to the blessing of Abraham.

5. **You are the seed of Abraham:**
   Christ has redeemed you from the curse of the Law so that the blessing of Abraham can come upon you who believe. Gal. 3:13-14. Every seed of Abraham is entitled to the blessing of Abraham. Gen. 12:3b…in him (Abraham) shall all the families of the earth be blessed.

6. **God is glorified in your prosperity:**
   Your prosperity brings delight to God. When God blesses a man, he has blessed a family and he has blessed a community. Many people through that man will also be a blessing. God blesses men so that they can be channel of blessing to others and this is what brings God glory.

7. **God does not want you to be poor:**

And there will I nourish thee; for yet [there are] five years of famine; lest thou, and thy household, and all that thou hast, come to poverty. Gen 45:11

God does not want you to be poor. Your poverty will not glorify God. The purpose of God's blessing is to remove the shame of poverty from your life. God don't want you to experience the hardship caused by poverty.

False Believe About Financial Prosperity

Financial Prosperity is having more than enough money to meet your needs in your life time and to help others achieve their dreams. Talking about financial prosperity, many people believe prosperity is a function of where you were born, who gave birth to you, the place you live and the people you are connected to. And some even considered it a product of being well academically educated. The truth is that none of these qualifies to make a man rich or prosper.

Prosperity is first a state of the mind. The scripture says, *as a man thinks in his heart so he his. Prov. 23:7a.* Any poor man who has a rich mind can turn his situation around because there is a rich man in every poor man. When there is mental poverty, there will be all round poverty. Lack of money and substance is not enough to qualify a man as poor, but poor mind-set and wrong believe about wealth is what makes a man really poor.

Anybody whose mind is open and is willing to learn the scriptural secret to financial breakthrough and practice them will surely experience financial fortune.

You can end your poverty if you can see that you have equal opportunity to become financially free like those who are financially free. God is not a respecter of any man. The day a man is ready for God to intervene in his matter and change his story, that will be a beginning of his prosperity.

Then Peter opened [his] mouth, and said, Of a truth I perceive that God is no respecter of persons: But in every nation he that feareth him, and worketh righteousness, is accepted with him. Acts 10:34-35.

God's arm is open to anyone who believes in his grace to change their lives. Believe in the working power of God and his word to change your situation. Don't settle for poverty, arise and shine into financial fortune. You can make it if you allow God to work with you and you in turn work with God.

5

Covenant Keys To Financial Breakthrough

Keep therefore the words of this covenant, and do them, that ye may prosper in all that ye do. Deut 29:9

Financial fortune is the dream of everyone. Thou financial fortune does not guarantee all round success. But it guarantees assurance of achieving many of your goals and vision. Money makes the world a better place to live. The secret of money is the ability to attract it enough. Some people don't just make money they attract and command it. You can attract money and also command it if you can understand the keys needed to do so. Money is a value for quality, idea, talent, skill, gifting, and smart-work.

Many people will actually wonder, can one be financially free by praying. They conclude that hard work and good opportunity will help you to gain financial freedom. That could be true to some extent. Prayer is the anti dot to every cause beyond human ability. Not everyone who works hard succeeds and not every business opportunity will give you financial freedom.

Keys To Financial Freedom

1. **The fear of the Lord:**
    This is a powerful key. God knows those who fear him and he will do anything to bless those who fear him.

Praise ye the LORD. **Blessed (is) the man that feareth the LORD,** *(that) delighteth greatly in his commandments. His seed shall be mighty upon the earth: the generation of the upright shall be blessed.* **Wealth and riches (shall be) in his house:** *and his righteousness endureth for ever. Ps. 112:1-3 (NIV).*

A man that fears the Lord is a treasure to the Lord. God will reveal his secret to those who fear him, even the secret of prosperity and he will lead them to where their will find lasting wealth.

2. The Love of God:

I love them that love me; and those that seek me early shall find me. Riches and honour (are) with me; (yea), durable riches and righteousness. That I may cause those that love me to inherit substance; and I will fill their treasures. Proverb. 17,18, 21 (NIV).

God loves those who love him. Love is a passionate desire for somebody. When you love God everything in you will reflect it. The way you speak about him, the way you worship him, the way you adore him, even the way you give to him. There is nothing too big in the eyes of a lover to give his love mate. And so there is nothing too big for God to give those who love him. The scripture is balanced on love. Lovers are entitled to the best from God. Be a lover of God.

3. Serving God:

If they obey and serve [him], they shall spend their days in prosperity, and their years in pleasures. Job 36:11

Serving God is commanded. Serving God is one of the ways God pours his blessing upon his people. He honors those who honor him in serving Him. God is honored by all the host of heavens and everything in creature. So when a man pleases God by serving Him, God in turn honors the man by remembering him. If you don't leave God's side God cannot leave your side.

4. **Obedience to the word of God:**

And it shall come to pass, if thou shalt hearken diligently unto the voice of the LORD thy God, to observe [and] to do all his commandments which I command thee this day, that the LORD thy God will set thee on high above all nations of the earth: And all these blessings shall come on thee, and overtake thee, if thou shalt hearken unto the voice of the LORD thy God. Deut. 28:1-2

Obedience is a key that opens the door of divine blessing. When we obey the word of God, God honors the word of our petitions and also fulfill his promises attached to obeying his word.

5. **Sacrificial Giving:**

But the king said to Araunah, **"No, I insist on buying it from you! I will not offer to the LORD my God burnt sacrifices that cost me nothing."** *So David bought the threshing floor and the oxen for fifty pieces of silver. 2Sam 24:24 (Net)*

David the King rejected the offer of receiving a free gift he wants to render to God as a sacrifice.

6. **Get a business or work to do that God can bless:**

[He that is] despised, and hath a servant, [is] better than he that honoureth himself, and lacketh bread. Prov. 12:9.

God needs something to bless. An idle man has no work worth blessing. Everyone that wants to enjoy the blessing of God needs to understanding that God blesses the work of your hand and in turn the work of your hand becomes a blessing to you.

7. **Be diligent in your work:**
He becometh poor that dealeth [with] a slack hand: but the hand of the diligent maketh rich. Prov. 10:4
Wealth [gotten] by vanity shall be diminished: but he that gathereth by labour shall increase. Prov. 13:11

A diligent man is a man committed to his work. Commitment to work requires hard work and smart work. As you work hard to make things happen you strategize to get favorable result. Diligence is a state of being unquestionably committed to what you are doing.

8. **Be Prayerful:**
Ask, and it shall be given you; seek, and ye shall find; knock, and it shall be opened unto you: Matt 7:7

Prayer of faith moves mountain. Pray is a spiritual force that has the power to change natural laws to your favor. To be prayerful means to be full of right prayer. Right prayer brings right result.

Summary

1. **Locate a powerful business idea:**
    Idea they say rules the world. A good business idea will open door to money making channel. A good idea is a capital in itself. Idea is a money magnet. Any idea God has laid in your heart to do, take your time to do it with all integrity and passion.

2. **Write good plans to execute it:**
    A good plan helps you to escape the trap of failure at all cost. The more clear your plan the more chances of early success in what you are doing. It is important you plan about everything. It is commonly said that, if you fail to plan, you have planned to fail. Planning is the art of taking your time to write out step by step of how to start, go about and execute you dreams. Planning is a road map to success.

3. **Acquire the knowledge of your trade:**
    Knowledge is power. If God says, my people are destroyed for lack of knowledge. Hosea 4:6. We need knowledge of how to do what we want to do. No company will employ a man who does not have the knowledge of his trade. You need to understand the place of knowledge in life.
    You can hardly succeed in the business you don't know anything about. You need adequate knowledge at your disposal to help in the exclusive execution of your vision.

4. **Be determined and focus:**

Determination is a passion booster. Determination is an evidence of your desire to break out of poverty. When you are determined you will be undivided. Anyone that must breakthrough must be determined and keep their focus on their goal.

5. **Walk in the covenant:**

The covenant is the instruction of God's word. Key your business to the covenant of blessing by paying your business tithe. *Malachi 3:9-11.*

Bring ye all the tithes into the storehouse, that there may be meat in mine house, and prove me now herewith, saith the LORD of hosts, if I will not open you the windows of heaven, and pour you out a blessing, that [there shall] not [be room] enough [to receive it]. And I will rebuke the devourer for your sakes, and he shall not destroy the fruits of your ground; neither shall your vine cast her fruit before the time in the field, saith the LORD of hosts. And all nations shall call you blessed: for ye shall be a delightsome land, saith the LORD of hosts. Mal 3:10-12

God will bless what you do based on partnering your business with him by walking according to his terms and condition. In doing this, God will rebuke every demon that wants to destroy your produce and make you run down. Powers of darkness will not have power over the work of your hands and your blessing will be evident to all.

6. **Have faith:**

Faith is one of the covenant keys to walking in prosperity. For without faith it is impossible to please God. Faith is an evidence of your assurance that the word of God will never fail concerning his promises of blessing those who yield to his word.

7. **Pray violently for breakthrough:**

   And he spake a parable unto them [to this end], that men ought always to pray, and not to faint; Luke 18:1

Pray against powers and forces that want you to serve under poverty. Pray against every obstacle, curses, spell that backs poverty and financial hardship in your life. Pray until financial breakthrough manifest in your life.

Section 2
Financial Breakthrough Prayers

This is a prayer section. As much as principles and action are needed, prayer is also needed. Read each prayer chapter carefully as that will give you clue why prayer is needed, and pray as demanded.

6
Oh Lord, Have Mercy On Me

Thou shalt arise, [and] have mercy upon Zion: for the time to favour her, yea, the set time, is come. Ps 102:13

Mercy is when God shows a man his compassion out of his goodness. Mercy is God's compassion. Mercy has no equal. When it is time for God to favor a man, it is in mercy He operates, so that every sin, judgment and reason for allegation can be overruled. Mercy is a great savior. The force of mercy is a major force in the requirement for breakthrough. When mercy is missing in the life of a man, he will experience first grade rejection and suffering. Mercy makes all the difference in your entire breakthrough prayer endeavour. A man minus God's mercy is equal to nothing; a man with God's mercy upon him is equal to greatness. You need the mercy of God to go places and receive something big from God.

Why many people never receive answers to their prayer is because they have not received the mercy of God. Mercy is a beauty of God upon a person that enables him to experience the goodness of God. Mercy is the custodian of favor. It ushers in favor, grace and glory.

For he saith to Moses, I will have mercy on whom I will have mercy, and I will have compassion on whom I will have compassion. So then [it is] not of him that willeth, nor of him that runneth, but of God that sheweth mercy. Rom 9:15-16

It is the mercy of God that makes the right opportunity to locate you and make your pursuit become fruitful. By strength shall no man prevail? You prevail by mercy. When mercy is at work, God is at work. It takes mercy to escape common punishment. Mercy is available for everyone but it is not on everyone. Mercy is for those who desire it. A man that lack mercy is not safe. Mercy qualifies, purifies, nullifies and glorifies the receiver.

You need to capitalize on the mercy of God if you expect anything great from God. Mercy makes all things possible for a man before God. And asking for mercy shows your level of dependence and humility before God. When God reveals himself in a man's situation through His mercy, it's for Him to show that he is merciful. Glory belongs to God for every major thing He does. David said, surely goodness and mercy shall follow me all the days of my life, and I will dwell in the house of the Lord forever. It takes mercy to make God available for you. You need to pay special attention to the issue of mercy. Many people will not amount to someone relevant in life until God shows them mercy. Mercy opens door to favor, breakthrough, wonders and many more.

Beloved, don't joke with the mercy of God; it is powerful enough to save you from the grip of poverty. Mercy will absolutely set you free from the bondage of hardship and poverty.

How to tap into mercy
1. Be saved. 1Pet. 2:10.
2. Ask for it. Matt.7:7
3. Show mercy to others. Matthew 5:7

Benefits of mercy
1. It makes God pays you attention. Luke 18:38-41
2. It rejoices over judgment. James 2:13
3. Mercy bails you out of problem. Isaiah 60:10
4. It can change your situation over-night.
5. Mercy brings restoration. Zech. 10:6
6. Mercy brings salvation. Titus 3:5
7. Mercy ushers in divine intervention for prosperity. Zech. 1:16-19.
8. Mercy gives you victory over your enemies. Ps. 143:12

Scriptural confession:
Hear me when I call, O God of my righteousness: thou hast enlarged me [when I was] in distress; have mercy upon me, and hear my prayer. Ps 4:1
Have mercy upon me, O LORD; for I [am] weak: O LORD, heal me; for my bones are vexed. Ps 6:2
Have mercy upon me, O LORD; consider my trouble [which I suffer] of them that hate me, thou that liftest me up from the gates of death: Ps 9:13

Hear, O LORD, [when] I cry with my voice: have mercy also upon me, and answer me. Ps 27:7

But as for me, my prayer [is] unto thee, O LORD, [in] an acceptable time: O God, in the multitude of thy mercy hear me, in the truth of thy salvation. Ps 69:13

Let us therefore come boldly unto the throne of grace, that we may obtain mercy, and find grace to help in time of need. Heb 4:16

Prayers
1. Oh Lord, show me mercy in Jesus name.

2. Oh Lord, make me a candidate of your mercy in Jesus name.

3. Oh Lord of mercy, arise in your mercy for my sake in the name of Jesus.

4. Door of mercy, open unto me in the name of Jesus.

5. Angel of mercy, appear and locate me in the name of Jesus.

6. Mercy for divine intervention, come into my life in the name of Jesus.

7. Canopy of mercy cover me in the name of Jesus.

8. My heaven of mercy, open by fire in the name of Jesus.

9. Oil of mercy from the throne of God, fall upon me in the name of Jesus.

10. Mercy of God, speak for me in the name of Jesus.

11. Mercy of the living God, flow into my life and bring in prosperity into my life in the name of Jesus.

7

Oh, Lord Endow Me With Power

But truly I am full of power by the spirit of the LORD, and of judgment, and of might, to declare unto Jacob his transgression, and to Israel his sin. Mic. 3:8

Power is a virtue. When the deposit of this virtue is in you it put you in authority and dominion. Faith works with the virtue of power in you. It takes faith plus power to move mountain. Faith without power will lead to expectation without manifestation. Every faith outcome is ignited by the force of power within.

Power give you edge over every adversary and give you dominion over them. It takes power to stand out. The power that comes from God is result oriented power. Anyone who wants positive outcome without delay needs power.

Case study:

And Jacob was left alone; and there wrestled a man with him until the breaking of the day.

And when he saw that he prevailed not against him, he touched the hollow of his thigh; and the hollow of Jacob's thigh was out of joint, as he wrestled with him.

And he said, Let me go, for the day breaketh. And he said, I will not let thee go, except thou bless me.

And he said unto him, What [is] thy name? And he said, Jacob.

And he said, Thy name shall be called no more Jacob, but Israel: for as a prince hast thou power with God and with men, and hast prevailed.

And Jacob asked [him], and said, Tell [me], I pray thee, thy name. And he said, Wherefore [is] it [that] thou dost ask after my name? And he blessed him there.
And Jacob called the name of the place Peniel: for I have seen God face to face, and my life is preserved. Gen 32:24-30.

Many factors contributed to the success of Jacob, one is the ability to see, that is vision. The man he wrestled with was an Angel, and not a man. He must have seen him through vision. Second thing is doggedness. He was a resilient and dogged man, who was determined and unstoppable. The most important factor to his victory was power.

*The LORD hath also a controversy with Judah, and will punish Jacob according to his ways; according to his doings will he recompense him. He took his brother by the heel in the womb, and by his strength he had power with God: Yea, **he had power over the angel,** and prevailed: he wept, and made supplication unto him: he found him [in] Bethel, and there he spake with us; Hosea 12:2-4*

Jacob prevailed because he had power with God by his strength. He has been empowered to see. The strength exhibited by him is the same thing as power. A physical man cannot use his physical strength to subdue an angel or a spirit being, except the man also has a spiritual weapon or power to do so. So the strength of Jacob was divine power. However, in these last days, the power of the Holy Ghost is available to make your victory over every problem of life a reality. Until power is poured from above through the Holy Spirit, life will remain a tragedy for man. It takes power to be free from all oppression of darkness, it takes power to possess your possession, it takes power to gain freedom and walk like a champion all around. Who is the source of this power? Holy Spirit!

The Holy Spirit is the power base of every believer.
But ye shall receive power, after that the Holy Ghost is come upon you: Acts 1:8a
But truly I am full of power by the spirit of the LORD, and of judgment, and of might, to declare unto Jacob his transgression, and to Israel his sin. Mic 3:8

Holy Spirit is the custodian of God's power, when you receive him, he empowers you. Your desire for Him makes all the difference in what you receive. Your encounter with the Holy Spirit is the beginning of your turn around. No one remains the same, encountering the Holy Spirit.

Jesus Christ has also given the assurance of the availability of this power for everyone who wants to overcome and succeed.

Why you need power?
1. You need power to make wealth. *Deut. 8:18*
2. You need power to change unwanted situation.*Mark 11:23*
3. You need power to remain on top of your game. *Micah 3:8*
4. You need power to generate positive result. *1Cor. 2:4*
5. You need power to subdue all your adversary. *Luke 10:19*

Why you need the Holy Spirit?
1. He is more than an Angel, He is God in You. 1John 4:13
2. He gives freedom. 2Cor. 3:17
3. He performs and transforms things supernaturally. John 1:12

4. He guides, instruct and direct to see a glorious result. Isaiah 30:21.
5. It has been promised by God. Act. 2:17
6. Power comes when the Holy Spirit comes. Act. 1:8

How To Receive Holy Spirit And Power

1. Accept Jesus into your life: John 1:12
   It takes salvation to receive the gift of the Holy Spirit.
2. Confess all your sins. Prov. 28:13
3. Consecrate yourself. 2Cor. 6:17
4. Ask for the power of the Holy Spirit. Luke 11:13
5. Have faith. Heb. 11:6

Scriptural confession:

If ye then, being evil, know how to give good gifts unto your children: how much more shall [your] heavenly Father give the Holy Spirit to them that ask him? Luke 11:13

But ye shall receive power, after that the Holy Ghost is come upon you: and ye shall be witnesses unto me both in Jerusalem, and in all Judaea, and in Samaria, and unto the uttermost part of the earth. Acts 1:8

Prayers

1. Oh Lord, sanctify me with your precious blood in the name of Jesus.
2. Anything in me that will resist the Holy Spirit and power, come out now in the name of Jesus.
3. Spirit of God fill me up in the name of Jesus.
4. Power of God for victory, my life is available; possess me in the name of Jesus.
5. Power of God from above, fall upon me in Jesus name.

8

Pulling Down Your
Foundation Of Poverty

If the foundations be destroyed, what can the righteous do? Ps 11:3

There are different kinds of foundations. Here we are addressing the foundation that has been connecting your destiny to poverty. Many people have a foundation that connects them to poverty, which is also making life miserable. A foundation of poverty is a faulty foundation, and it cannot support financial fortune, until that foundation is pulled down and another one is rebuilt. Your foundation is your land of nativity and what is obtainable in the family you were born into.

What is an evil foundation?
An evil foundation is an origin with evil record, evil works that is left over by past generation with the consequences on the next generation. It is a foundation that is passed on from past generation to the present generation. Your foundation is the point you originated from, your DNA source, your bloodline, your hereditary, where your destiny was connected, the ancestors that left over their names for you is your foundation. Every root of poverty will give birth to the fruit of poverty. It is important to deal ruthlessly with every root of evil foundation that is connected to poverty so that you can gain freedom from financial oppression.

If the foundation is destroyed, what can the righteous do? Ps. 11:3. Your foundation is stronger than you. It decides your fortune and misfortune. It is the spiritual remote control of your life. It has full control over your life, until that faulty foundation is pulled down and a good one is erected there will not be upward progress. Whatever is obtainable in your foundation will be obtainable in your life. The value of a land is not just by the weed that grows on it, not by the rock, but by the mineral resources. The resources there are the worth of that land. You are like the material product of your foundation.

There are several factors that establish such a foundation,
1. Idolatry
2. Ancestral curse
3. Ancestral Evil covenants and it consequences
4. Unfulfilled of vows.
5. Rituals and evil sacrifice that was carried out in your background.
6. Past mistakes and errors.

How to overcome this kind of foundation
1. Give your life to Jesus. John 1:12
2. Pray violently. James 5:16
3. Engage in 21 days fasting. Ezra 8:21-23
4. Undergo deliverance. 2tim. 4:18

Your foundation and you
- You are the offshoot of your foundation, whether good or bad.

- You are what your foundation birthed.

- There are principalities and powers in your foundation that recognize you and are tied to you one way or the other.

- Work on your faulty foundation to have a better life.

Scriptural confession:

(For the weapons of our warfare [are] not carnal, but mighty through God to the pulling down of strong holds;) Casting down imaginations, and every high thing that exalteth itself against the knowledge of God, and bringing into captivity every thought to the obedience of Christ; 2Cor 10:4-5.

Prayer

1. Evil foundation of my father's house and mother's house that is connected to my life be destroyed by fire in the name of Jesus.
2. Every foundational networks and attachment to my life be destroyed in the name of Jesus.
3. Every root and tentacles of evil foundation be dismantled in the name of Jesus.
4. Powers and principalities controlling my foundation, release me and die in the name of Jesus.
5. Evil Powers operating at the root of my foundation die in Jesus name.
6. Evil covenant of my foundation supporting poverty, break by fire in the name of Jesus.
7. Evil voices speaking in my foundation against my life be silenced in the name of Jesus.
8. Evil foundation and it altar scatter propagating poverty against me, be consumed by fire in Jesus name.
9. Every foundation of poverty standing in my life, collapse in Jesus name.
10. Covenant keeping powers in my foundation sustaining poverty, die by fire in the name of Jesus.
11. Every foundational forces holding me back from becoming what God has created me to be, release me and disappear in the mighty name of Jesus.

12. My foundation, release me by fire in the name of Jesus.

13. My foundation, release my prosperity in the name of Jesus.

14. My foundation, vomit my riches in the name of Jesus.

15. Every foundational power that wants to keep me in perpetual bondage of poverty, release me and die in the name of Jesus.

16. Every foundational evil altar in my life catch-fire in the name of Jesus.

17. I rebuild a new foundation of prosperity in Jesus name.

9

Destroying The Altar of Poverty

*But thus shall ye deal with them; ye shall destroy their altars, and break
down their images, and cut down their groves, and burn their graven images
with fire. Deut 7:5*

Altar is a point of contact between the physical and the spiritual. Altar is a place where sacrifice of all kinds is made. An evil altar is a place where evil are decided over the destiny of people. Evil foundational altars can be raised against people's destiny and financial breakthrough. When altars are raised against people's finance, every effort to gather, will the aborted. Every opportunity that can bring in money and financial breakthrough will be blocked by the powers that have been given the assignment on the altars over the destinies of others.

Evil altars are controlled by demonic spirit. The spirits on the altars are the powers that operate on that altar and have made that altar the place of their habitation. They are diverse operation of principalities and powers from the podium of evil altars. If an altar of poverty has been raised, demon of poverty will be summoned to keep tab on the person the altar is raised against. Evil altars have to be destroyed.

Powers that operate evil altars
1. Witchcraft power
2. Marine powers
3. Familiar spirit
4. Territorial spirit

5. Foundational powers
6. Occultic powers
7. Personal wickedness altars
8. And all other demonic powers

All those powers operating this altar can use the altar to finish the financial destiny of any business and individual.

How to overcome altars of poverty
1. Abide in Christ.
2. Make possible amendment
3. Pray and pull down the altar
4. Sow a seed into a church for restoration

Scriptural Confession
The earth [is] the LORD'S, and the fullness thereof; the world, and they that dwell therein. For he hath founded it upon the seas, and established it upon the floods.
Who shall ascend into the hill of the LORD? or who shall stand in his holy place?
He that hath clean hands, and a pure heart; who hath not lifted up his soul unto vanity, nor sworn deceitfully. He shall receive the blessing from the LORD, and righteousness from the God of his salvation. This [is] the generation of them that seek him, that seek thy face, O Jacob. Selah. Lift up your heads, O ye gates; and be ye lift up, ye everlasting doors; and the King of glory shall come in. Who [is] this King of glory? The LORD strong and mighty, the LORD mighty in battle. Lift up your heads, O ye gates; even lift [them] up, ye everlasting doors; and the King of glory shall come in. Who is this King of glory? The LORD of hosts, he [is] the King of glory. Selah. Psalm 24:1-10.

Prayers

1. Every altars of poverty fighting my destiny, catch-fire in the name of Jesus.

2. Every power appointed on evil altars against my finances, I bind you in the name of Jesus, I command your operation to cease in the name of Jesus.

3. Every token that has been given on any evil altar against my financial fortune, be destroyed in the name of Jesus.

4. Any evil sacrifice that has been given or placed on any evil altar against my business, works and financial fortune, be destroyed by the blood of Jesus.

5. Every stronghold of poverty erected against me on evil altars, be pulled down in the name of Jesus.

6. Every evil oath, covenant and decrees made on evil altar against my financial breakthrough, break in the name of Jesus.

7. Every covenant fighting my prosperity, break in the name of Jesus.

8. Any evil altar that has been specially raised against my life, business and finances be destroyed in the name of Jesus.

9. Operation of evil altars against my business and finance be destroyed by fire in the name of Jesus.

10. Oh Lord, redeem my financial fortune in the name of Jesus.

10

Breaking Ancestral Curse Of Poverty

And Jacob called unto his sons, and said, Gather yourselves together, that I may tell you [that] which shall befall you in the last days. Gather yourselves together, and hear, ye sons of Jacob; and hearken unto Israel your father. Reuben, thou [art] my firstborn, my might, and the beginning of my strength, the excellency of dignity, and the excellency of power: Gen 29:32; Unstable as water, thou shalt not excel; because thou wentest up to thy father's bed; then defiledst thou [it]: he went up to my couch. Gen 49:1-4.

Reuben was cursed, every tribe that emerge out of Reuben never made it. They suffered poverty and their glory was silenced. Curse is a destroying force. It destroy good prospect and weaken the strength of the mighty.

Now the sons of Reuben the firstborn of Israel, (for he [was] the firstborn; but, forasmuch as he defiled his father's bed, his birthright was given unto the sons of Joseph the son of Israel: and the genealogy is not to be reckoned after the birthright. 1Chr 5:1

Curse is a negative word that is issued with a wicked intention to cause havoc to people's life and destiny. Curse can move on from one generation to another till the fourth generation. If a curse is not stopped, it will continue to operate freely.

Ancestral curse is the curse that operates from a person's ancestral line down to the present generation, and it is still operating. When this curse is in place, it will be caging the financial glory of everyone born into that family, except the person that is delivered from the operation of that curse. Curse operate freely, it does not need invitation to operate. As long as someone is connected by birth, blood, genealogy to the lineage where the curse is raging, they become a carrier of that curse. Curse does not have respect for a person, be it black, white, Caucasian. Albino, whoever you may be, wherever you may be born. But what is most important is to identify the curse and terminate its existing operation over your life.

When ancestral curse of poverty is at work in a family, everyone born in that family will suffer uniform financial hardship. It will be obvious that poverty is in charge in such a family. All effort and input they make in that family to strike financial rest will be impossible. When ancestral curse of poverty is at work in a family, no matter the academic laurel, no matter the opportunity any member of that family may have, it will not amount into a major financial success.

Causes of ancestral curses
1. Idolatry
2. Killing for ritual
3. Betrayal
4. Disobedience to God.
5. Wrong practices
6. wickedness
7. Stealing. etc

Way out
1. Repentance from those things
2. Pray for mercy
3. Deliverance and restoration prayers

4. Serving God faithfully

Scriptural Declaration

Christ hath redeemed us from the curse of the law, being made a curse for us: for it is written, Cursed [is] every one that hangeth on a tree:
That the blessing of Abraham might come on the Gentiles through Jesus Christ; that we might receive the promise of the Spirit through faith. Gal 3:13-14.

The word of the LORD came unto me again, saying, What mean ye, that ye use this proverb concerning the land of Israel, saying, The fathers have eaten sour grapes, and the children's teeth are set on edge? [As] I live, saith the Lord GOD, ye shall not have [occasion] any more to use this proverb in Israel. Ezek 18:1-3

Produce your cause, saith the LORD; bring forth your strong [reasons], saith the King of Jacob. Isa 41:21.

Prayers

1. Oh Lord, forgive and cancel all ancestral sins and mistaken speaking in my life in Jesus name.
2. Oh Lord, let your mercy overrule every ancestral judgment upon my destiny in Jesus name.
3. Oh Lord, let your blood silence every foundational voices and speak in my favor in the name of Jesus.
4. Blood of Jesus redeem me from every ancestral curses in Jesus name.
5. Any curse working against my financial success, be cancelled by the blood of Jesus.
6. I release myself from every ancestral curse of poverty in the name of Jesus.

7. Every curse of begging to survive in my life, be broken in the name of Jesus.

8. Every curse of rising and falling in my life be broken in Jesus name.

9. Every curse of suffering and hardship be broken in Jesus name.

10. Every curse of rising early and falling later in life be broken in Jesus name.

11. Every curse of failure at the edge of breakthrough in my life be broken in Jesus name.

12. Every curse of backwardness and non-achievement in my life be broken in Jesus name.

13. Every curse of as you are born that is how you will die, be cancelled in Jesus name.

14. Every curse attached to a condition, unless or except in my life be broken and cancelled by the blood of Jesus in the name of Jesus.

15. Every curse of battle at key point in my life be cancelled in Jesus name.

16. Every curse of shame and reproach in my life be cancelled in Jesus name.

17. Every curse of denial of good things and rejection be broken and cancelled in Jesus name.

18. Every known and unknown curse backing up poverty, hardship, suffering, difficulty in my life, marriage and work of my hands be broken and totally cancelled by the blood of Jesus in Jesus name.

19. Every spirit assigned against ancestral curse in my life, I terminate your assignment and operation with the blood of Jesus.

20. I recover back all my lost year in Jesus name.

21. I decree and declare, I am blessed, I am not cursed in Jesus name.
22. I turn all curses to blessing in Jesus name.
23. Every identity of curses in my life, be cancelled in Jesus name.
24. Any accursed name I am bearing affecting my life, I cancel it in Jesus name.
25. Any accurse location affecting my financial flow and success, I command the curse to be destroyed by the blood of Jesus.
26. Every stronghold of curse in my life, break by fire in the name of Jesus.
27. Every agent of darkness planted in my life to keep me under curse and poverty, I am no more your candidate, release me by the authority in Jesus name and die by fire.
28. Anointing of blessing, fall upon me in Jesus name.
29. Anointing of favor fall upon me in Jesus name.
30. Anointing for help and helpers fall upon me in Jesus name.
31. Anointing for open doors fall upon me in Jesus name.
32. Anointing for 24hours miracle of help and financial breakthrough, fall upon me in Jesus name.

11
Arresting The Spirit of Lack and Poverty

*The rich man's wealth [is] his strong city: the destruction of the poor [is]
their poverty. Prov. 10:15*

Behind every problem known to man, there is a spirit sponsoring and supervising it. Different kind of demonic spirits operate in the world and lives of people to keep them in the bondage of their problem. The major assignment of this spirits is to perform the name they bear in the life of their victim. If it is infirmity, the victim will be afflicted with sickness, if it is the spirit of limitation the person will remain limited without going beyond the level set for him, if it is stagnation, the person will remain in one spot, and if it is lack, it will bring scarcity of material and financial needs in that life, and if it is poverty, it will make the victim so poor that all that he has will not be enough to sustain him all the time. It takes authority in the name of Jesus to deal with the spirits and be free from their dominion and operation in their victim's life.

Many people cannot explain why they are born into poverty. Though, being born into poverty is not the reason why you should remain in poverty. Poverty is a tragedy of the poor, opportunity of the rich. Everyone that was once poor can become rich, because in every poor man is a rich man. No poor idea. One idea that comes out of you can turn around your life forever.

There are several factors that control and prolong poverty in people's life. One of it is the spirit behind poverty and the mindset that sees poverty as an inheritance. The confidence we have when we pray is that the living God we serve answers prayer. And the case of poverty is not a hard one for him to solve.

Many people are under the captivity of the spirit of poverty and yet looking for a breakthrough. The more they try to escape the more they go into deeper captivity of the spirit of lack and poverty.

There is a spirit that has been assigned to keep people in the bondage of poverty. Many people operate under the spell of this demonic spirit, and they need to be delivered. Until the spirit of lack and poverty set a man free, he will remain in the stronghold of lack.

As you pray against this spirit, I want you to have this understanding. If a poor man sees himself as being poor he will remain poor, but if a poor man keep seeing riches and prosperity in himself and dreams it, and work towards it, he will become rich because in every poor man is a rich man.

How To Be Delivered
1. Believe in the power of God to deliver. Matt. 28:18
2. Understand that prosperity is your inheritance in Christ. 2Cor. 8:9
3. Pray violently to be delivered. Joel 2:32

Scriptural Confession:
And it shall come to pass, [that] whosoever shall call on the name of the LORD shall be delivered: for in mount Zion and in Jerusalem shall be

deliverance, as the LORD hath said, and in the remnant whom the LORD shall call. Joel 2:32

Our soul is escaped as a bird out of the snare of the fowlers: the snare is broken, and we are escaped.
Our help [is] in the name of the LORD, who made heaven and earth. Ps 124:7-8

Prayers

1. Spirit of poverty I bind you in the name of Jesus, release me and let me go in Jesus name.
2. Spirit of lack and poverty release me forever and die in you in Jesus name.
3. Spirit of lack of help and helpers, I bind you in Jesus name.
4. Every power frustrating my effort, release me and die in Jesus name.
5. Any power and spirit assigned to keep me in perpetual bondage of poverty release me and die in Jesus name.
6. Any spirit responsible for poverty in my life, release me and die in the name of Jesus.
7. Any legal ground that this spirit has over my life, I break and destroy it in the name of Jesus.
8. I lose myself from every spirit holding me down to poverty in the name of Jesus.
9. Every state of poverty in my life, change by fire in the name of Jesus.
10. I cancel my name from the list of poverty forever in the name of Jesus.
11. Every agenda of poverty over my life and family be frustrated and destroyed in the name of Jesus.

12. Every program of poverty for my life, be aborted by fire in the name of Jesus.

13. I break loose from poverty from today in the name of Jesus.

12

Breaking The Yoke Of Indebtedness

The rich ruleth over the poor, and the borrower [is] servant to the lender.
Prov. 22:7

Every debtor is a poor man. Every debtor just has an image but no credibility before the lender. All that he enjoys is based on the platform of debt. Every debtor is a servant to his lender, be it an organization or individual.

Borrowing and taking loan can become a pattern that will be difficult to break. And as it may be, that will be a medium of paying a large percent of the business profit to the lender, and still owing more. Until the yoke is broken, the borrower will end in debt. Many great business men has committed suicide because of debt, many suffer mental and psychological breakdown because of debt.

Debt is a disease that has to be terminating by breaking every yoke propelling it. God wants to bless you and your business in such a way that borrowing will be far from you. He wants to bless you and cause you to lend to nations. God has the agenda set.

The LORD shall open unto thee his good treasure, the heaven to give the rain unto thy land in his season, and to bless all the work of thine hand: and thou shalt lend unto many nations, and thou shalt not borrow. Deut 28:12

Yoke is anything that ties a man down to a particular negative situation. Yokes is bondage, yoke brings stagnation, frustration and repetition of failure. Yoke has to be broken and destroyed for freedom to be attained.

For it shall come to pass in that day, saith the LORD of hosts, [that] I will break his yoke from off thy neck, and will burst thy bonds, and strangers shall no more serve themselves of him: Jer 30:8

God is a yoke breaker, and he has given you the authority in the name of Jesus to destroy and break yokes. Until the yoke is broken, there cannot be freedom from that particular bondage the yoke is established to perform.

Disadvantages Of Borrowing

As it has an advantage, it also has a greater disadvantage.

1. It makes you miserable when you cannot pay back.
2. It causes division of focus.
3. It brings unnecessary fear and pressure when the lender comes knocking.
4. It makes you restless and seeking for others help.
5. It can make you take regrettable decision just to bail out yourself.
6. It can bring loses.
7. It will make you lie.
8. It brings shame and reproach.
9. It brings low self-esteem.
10. It can run down a business and life.
11. It is not good for poor financial manager.

How To Be Free From Borrowing And Debt

Many people are in indebted because they borrow for business and other personal use.

1. Maintain a covenant practice of giving.
2. Start with what you have.
3. Project higher, but from down to the top.
4. Have a small financial goal and multiplication plan.
5. Create a platform for investment into your ideas and business.
6. Stop thinking that the only way out is getting loan.
7. Don't create a false image, what you are not up to, don't try to borrow to make yourself so.
8. Pray to receive the grace to put an end to it and find greater help of God to bail you out.

Scriptural confession

And it shall come to pass in that day, [that] his burden shall be taken away from off thy shoulder, and his yoke from off thy neck, and the yoke shall be destroyed because of the anointing. Isa 10:27

For now will I break his yoke from off thee, and will burst thy bonds in sunder. Nah 1:13

For it shall come to pass in that day, saith the LORD of hosts, [that] I will break his yoke from off thy neck, and will burst thy bonds, and strangers shall no more serve themselves of him: Jer 30:8.

Prayer

1. Every power that wants to make me a debtor, release me now in the name of Jesus.
2. Every yoke of debt in my life, break in the name of Jesus.

3. Every curse of borrowing and debt in my life be cancelled and destroyed in the name of Jesus.

4. Every urgent situation that is arising seasonal pushing me into loans expire in the name of Jesus.

5. Every inherited pattern of debt in my life and family, be destroyed in the name of Jesus.

6. I receive grace to overcome borrowing and debt lifestyle in the name of Jesus.

7. I break every mindset of borrowing in me, be cancelled in the name of Jesus.

8. Power for divine provision, my life is available possess me in the name of Jesus.

9. Every repeated circle of debt and borrowing that has been programmed into my life be broken and destroyed permanently in the mighty name of Jesus.

10. Anointing for more than enough possess me in the name of Jesus.

13

Victory over The Enemy of Your Progress

Thine hand shall be lifted up upon thine adversaries, and all thine enemies shall be cut off. Mic. 5:9

Victory means to overcome your enemy. You cannot be a victor if you have not overcome. And every victory is kick-started by a fight of determination to bring an end to oppression. You have to be determined to confront and conquer all the enemies of your progress.

Enemy of progress cage people and stop them from manifesting greatness. Enemy wants to do everything possible to make your effort a waste. Enemies are the powers behind failure. It does not matter the greatness of a man's idea, his chances and opportunities, if certain enemy has set himself to turn against your progress, he will do everything humanly and diabolically possible to hinder the man's progress.

The bible said, *for they sleep not, except they have done mischief; and their sleep is taken away, unless they cause some to fall. vs 16.*

Your enemies are bent on fulfilling their mission at whatever it will cost them. They will not sleep, they will not slumber, all their thinking is how they can stop you and put an end to your smile. That is the reason you must not go to sleep until you deal with your enemy.

Your enemies act like that, *because they have eaten the bread of wickedness, and drink the wine of violence. vs.17*

Your enemy's spirit and soul has been polluted with the seed of wickedness and are intoxicated with the wine of violence. And so a drunk man cannot recover from his drunkenness until the wine comes down, likewise your enemy will not retreat from their wickedness until they have accomplished their aims.

Your enemy does not want you to come out in flying colors. Your enemy wants your downfall, calamity, and creates problems for you. Enemies are meant to be confronted, not to be feared. Any thing that stands as an enemy of progress against your warfare don't want you to succeed easily. He wants life to be permanently miserable for you, but through prayer fervent prayers your enemies shall be defeated.

Enemy of progress has been programmed to cause hindrances to progress. Enemy can be programmed to work deliberately against you. Don't ever think you don't have an enemy. Everyone has an enemy…Jesus said. …*And a man's foes [shall be] they of his own household. Matt 10:36.*

Don't be afraid of confronting your enemy, your enemies are cheap to be defeated when you are in God and you are totally determined to defeat them with all the spiritual arsenal in your custody. Moreover, God has promised to fight for you.

Ye are of God, little children, and have overcome them: because greater is he that is in you, than he that is in the world. 1John 4:4.

Why You Must Deal With Your Enemies

1. They can stand as obstacles against your opportunities: 2cor.16:9
2. Enemy can make a mess of your life. Ps. 143:3
3. Enemy can set you up to kill you. John 10:10
4. Enemy can sell you out. Luke 22:47-48
5. Enemy cause oppression: Exod.3:9
6. Enemy can destroy all you have worked for in a jivy. John 10:10

Scriptural confessions

For the oppression of the poor, for the sighing of the needy, now will I arise, saith the LORD; I will set [him] in safety [from him that] puffeth at him. Ps 12:5

Out of the mouth of babes and sucklings hast thou ordained strength because of thine enemies, that thou mightest still the enemy and the avenger. Ps 8:2

So shall they fear the name of the LORD from the west, and his glory from the rising of the sun. When the enemy shall come in like a flood, the Spirit of the LORD shall lift up a standard against him. Isa 59:19

Behold, I give unto you power to tread on serpents and scorpions, and over all the power of the enemy: and nothing shall by any means hurt you. Luke 10:19

Prayers

1. Powers assigned to frustrate my life, somersault and die in Jesus name.
2. Every physical and spiritual enemy cultivating evil in my life, release me and die in Jesus name.
3. Every satanic propaganda against my breakthrough, scatter by fire in Jesus name.
4. Every forces of hell assigned to oppress me and keep me in perpetual bondage, scatter and die in Jesus name.

5. Every hidden enemy of my breakthrough be exposed and disgraced in Jesus name.

6. Every unfriendly enemy be exposed and disgraced in Jesus name.

7. Every household enemy be exposed and disgraced in Jesus name.

8. Every church hold enemy be exposed and disgraced in Jesus name.

9. Every business enemy be exposed and disgraced in Jesus name.

10. Every devourer be exposed and disgraced in Jesus name.

11. Every operation of the enemy against my breakthrough and financial turnaround be terminated in the name of Jesus.

12. Every violent and aggressive enemy, die by fire in the name of Jesus.

13. Every unrepentant enemy of my life and breakthrough, be exposed, paralyzed and die in the name of Jesus.

14. Anger of God fall upon my enemy in the name of Jesus.

15. Fires of God consume all my enemies in the name of Jesus.

16. Judgments of God fall upon all my enemies in the name of Jesus.

17. Arrows of God strike down my enemies and evil allies in the name of Jesus.

18. Thunder of God scatter the gathering of my enemies in the name of Jesus.

19. Sword of God, cut down my enemies in the name of Jesus.

20. Power of God locate my enemies and demobilize them in the name of Jesus.

21. Every evil works the enemy has done against my life, breakthrough and finance, be exposed and destroyed in the name of Jesus.

22. Every perfected work of the enemy against my life and finance, scatter in the name of Jesus.

23. Every burial ground of virtue, glory and good things the enemy has dug for my treasures, be destroyed by the spiritual earthquake of God in Jesus name.

24. Every belly of darkness where my riches is being swallowed up, burst and catch fire in the name of Jesus.

25. Every warehouse of my enemy where they are caging my treasure, riches, benefits, release my benefits and explode by the thunder power of the Holy Ghost in the name of Jesus.

26. Every wall of hindrance and limitation the enemy has built around my life and breakthrough be destroyed by fire in the name of Jesus.

27. Every mountain of difficulty that has been erected against me, disappear by the authority in the mighty name of Jesus.

28. Holy Ghost bomb, explode all the gadget, devices and weapons the enemy are engaging against my life and breakthrough in Jesus name.

29. Any evil pot the enemy has caged my glory, riches, money, prosperity, myself, explode by fire and release all that pertains to me in the name of Jesus.

30. I receive absolute deliverance from the enemy in the name of Jesus.

31. I receive total victory over all the enemies of my work, glory, progress and financial freedom in the name of Jesus.

14
Breaking The Chains Of Poverty

Then the chief captain came near, and took him, and commanded [him] to be bound with two chains; and demanded who he was, and what he had done.
Acts 21:33.

What is obtainable in the physical world is obtainable in the spiritual world. As many as are bound with evil chains has been enslaved to serve money till they die.

An evil chain is an invisible chain of darkness that can be used to tie a man down, tie is legs down, tie his business down, tie his finance down, or tie down one thing or the other that will profits him greatly. Evil chains are not chains you can see with your physical eyes, or feel like a physical chain. The only thing is that whatever is tied down will remain in one spot.

When enemy ties down a man and put him under surveillance, they have caged his destiny under a serious bondage. Such a person cannot amount to anything good, and cannot achieve anything tangible, but this moment shall the Lord deliver you as you pray in Jesus name.

Anyone tied down with this chain will remain in the same spot forever, until God has mercy on him and deliver him by his power.

For if God spared not the angels that sinned, but cast [them] down to hell, and delivered [them] into chains of darkness, to be reserved unto judgment; 2Pet 2:4.

Note this, if a person's business, finance or hands are spiritual chained, even if he dies unfulfilled, he will remain tied forever. You are not born to be tied. You are a free man. Christ has made you free from all evil chains. It is slaved that are chained and you are not a slave, break free.

Here is the goodnews

Stand fast therefore in the liberty wherewith Christ hath made us free, and be not entangled again with the yoke of bondage. Gal 5:1

God setteth the solitary in families: he bringeth out those which are bound with chains: but the rebellious dwell in a dry [land]. Ps 68:6.

Understand that everything about a man can be chained, money can be caged, health can be chained, human spirit can be chained, business and marriage can be chained, but God can lose you from all evil chains.

Peter therefore was kept in prison: but prayer was made without ceasing of the church unto God for him. And when Herod would have brought him forth, the same night Peter was sleeping between two soldiers, bound with two chains: and the keepers before the door kept the prison. And, behold, the angel of the Lord came upon [him], and a light shined in the prison: and he smote Peter on the side, and raised him up, saying, Arise up quickly. And his chains fell off from [his] hands. Acts 12:5-7

God delivered peter from prison and broke off the chains tying him down and he went free. The same is about to happen to you as you pray with faith and authority in Jesus name.

Scriptural confession

And from the days of John the Baptist until now the kingdom of heaven suffereth violence, and the violent take it by force. Matt 11:12

Verily I say unto you, Whatsoever ye shall bind on earth shall be bound in heaven: and whatsoever ye shall loose on earth shall be loosed in heaven. Matt 18:18

Prayers

1. Oh Lord, have mercy on me and set me free in Jesus name.
2. Every cord of poverty, holding me captive, loose me and let me go in the name of Jesus.
3. Every chains of poverty, tying me down, break by fire in the name of Jesus.
4. Mantle of power and fire I am available, fall on me in Jesus name.
5. Every chains of darkness tying me down in the name of Jesus break by fire.
6. Every evil chains tying my money down in the name of Jesus break by fire.
7. Any evil chain tying down my business in the name of Jesus break by fire.
8. Any evil chain tying down my glory in the name of Jesus break by fire.
9. Any evil chain tying down my help and helpers in the name of Jesus break by fire.
10. Any handler of evil chains in my life, fall down and die in the name of Jesus.

11. Wherever I have been chained, oh Lord go there and lose me free in the name of Jesus.
12. Wherever my money is tied down, oh Lord, release my money in the name of Jesus.
13. Every divination and enchantment that has been engaged in chaining me, lose your hold in the name of Jesus.
14. Anything tying me down, release me and break by fire in the name of Jesus.
15. Anything tying down my finance and breakthrough, lose it and be destroyed in the name of Jesus.
16. Anything tying down my business, break by fire in the name of Jesus.
17. Any area I am tied, and my finance, I command freedom in the name of Jesus.

15

Stopping The Operation Of Devourers

Be sober, be vigilant; because your adversary the devil, as a roaring lion, walketh about, seeking whom he may devour: 1Pet 5:8

Devouring spirit is spirit that devours good things. These spirits are called devourers. Mal. 3:11. The Devourer are the powers that consumes resources and make people to labour in vain. Devourer ensures people labor and never gathers what they labored for. Devouring powers ensures that all that pertains to their prey is consumed. They devour anything that can prosper their victim. Riches can be devoured.

He hath swallowed down riches, and he shall vomit them up again: God shall cast them out of his belly. Job 20:15

Devourers are the spirit that cause compulsory loses or mismanagement of funds. Where ever they enter, they empty every good thing available till there is nothing left to fall back on. Devouring spirit unleashed over a business will run down the business and it resources. Devourer creates a problem that will involve wasting of money, and resources without meaningful solution. When the spirit is arrested then wastage will cease.

And the children of Israel did evil in the sight of the LORD: and the LORD delivered them into the hand of Midian seven years. And the hand of Midian prevailed against Israel: [and] because of the Midianites the children of Israel made them the dens which [are] in the mountains, and caves, and strong holds. And [so] it was, when Israel had sown, that the Midianites came up, and the Amalekites, and the children of the east, even they came up against them; And they encamped against them, and destroyed the increase of the earth, till thou come unto Gaza, and left no sustenance for Israel, neither sheep, nor ox, nor ass. For they came up with their cattle and their tents, and they came as grasshoppers for multitude; [for] both they and their camels were without number: and they entered into the land to destroy it. And Israel was greatly impoverished because of the Midianites; and the children of Israel cried unto the LORD. Judg. 6:1-6.

The Midianites are devourers. The scriptures noted that when the Israelites has sown, when it is time to harvest the Midianites will come and destroy all their increase and leave them nothing, and they will become stranded of food, money and trade. They were impoverished. The spirit of devourer makes their victim to be impoverished, to labor and lack, to borrow and end in loses, to plan and fail, to build for another to inhabit.

Devouring spirit causes
1. Back to square one situation.
2. It causes frustration and pain.
3. It makes her victim to become poor and poorer in substance.
4. It causes total loses.
5. It makes their victim to labor in vain.
6. It target time of harvest, blessing and breakthrough and block or divert their expectation elsewhere.
7. It makes their victim to wait for breakthrough in vain.
8. It makes their victim to be a debtor and put them in shame.

How To Overcome Devouring Spirit

1. Give your life to Jesus. Roms. 8:1-2.
2. Pay your tithe promptly. Mal. 3:10-11
3. Pray prevailing prayers to end their operation. Ps. 34: 17
4. Engage fasting to war against that spirit. Matt. 17:21

Scriptural confession:

Wherefore God also hath highly exalted him, and given him a name which is above every name: That at the name of Jesus every knee should bow, of [things] in heaven, and [things] in earth, and [things] under the earth; And [that] every tongue should confess that Jesus Christ [is] Lord, to the glory of God the Father. Phil 2:9-11.

Giving thanks unto the Father, which hath made us meet to be partakers of the inheritance of the saints in light: Who hath delivered us from the power of darkness, and hath translated [us] into the kingdom of his dear Son: In whom we have redemption through his blood, [even] the forgiveness of sins: Col 1:12-14.

And the God of peace shall bruise Satan under your feet shortly. The grace of our Lord Jesus Christ [be] with you. Amen. Rom 16:20.

Prayers

1. Oh Lord, have mercy on me and bail me out in Jesus name.
2. Every legal ground of devouring spirit in my life and finance, be destroyed in the name of Jesus.
3. I bind every devouring spirit operating in the vicinity of my business and finance in the name of Jesus.
4. Every devouring sickness in my life, come out and die in the name of Jesus.

5. Every devouring problem in my life and business, come out and die in the name of Jesus.

6. Every devouring powers in my life and business, I command you to surrender to the name of Jesus and catch fire in the name of Jesus.

7. Every covenant binding my business and finance to devouring be destroyed in the name of Jesus.

8. Every assignment of devouring spirit in my life and business be terminated in the name of Jesus.

9. Every gathering and fellowship of devourers in my life, receive fire and scatter by fire in the name of Jesus.

10. Every arrow of devourer, fired into my finance and business, I command you in the name of Jesus, come out and catch fire in the name of Jesus.

11. Every demon on assignment to waste my resources and consume my goods and money, be arrested by the fire of the Holy Ghost and die in the name of Jesus.

12. Any animal that has been programmed to devour my money and business in the dream or physical be arrested and die in the name of Jesus.

13. Any dream I have ever had or dreamt that activate the operation of loses and waste in my life and business and finance, be aborted in the name of Jesus.

14. Any agent of devourer in my life, and business be exposed and destroyed in the name of Jesus.

15. Any staff that represent devourer in my organization, be exposed and disgraced in the name of Jesus.

16. Any family member that is operating as a devourer against my life, business and resources be exposed and disgraced by fire in the name of Jesus.

17. Powers from hell stationed against my financial flow and blessing, receive fire and die in the name of Jesus.

18. Holy Ghost fire, expose and consume every devouring agent in my life, business, career, finance in the name of Jesus.
19. Every operation of devourer in my life and business, expire in the mighty name of Jesus.
20. I call for the angel of increase and multiplication to take over my business, finance and life in the name of Jesus.
21. Favor that brings total restoration rest upon my finance and business in the name of Jesus.
22. Every habitation of devourer in my life and organization, catch fire in the name of Jesus.
23. Any vow and oaths made against be to sustain a lifetime operation of devourer, be destroyed by the blood of Jesus.
24. I command my deliverance from devourer operation in the name of Jesus.
25. I command the restoration of all my loses in the name of Jesus.
26. Every loopholes and doors that has been opened for loses in my business and finance, I shut it up in the mighty name of Jesus.

16
Silencing The Accusers Of Your Prosperity

Accusers are condemning voices. They are voices that kill good things, steal good things, stops and divert good things away from their victim. There are too many invisible voices in operation in people's life that is challenging their ware fare. Accuser condemns, denies and hinders good things. Accusing voices turns the heart of the helper away from those whom they are meant to help. Accusing voices are warning and treating spiritual and physical voices that warns and threatens people from helping their victim. Accusing voices are attacking voices that can attack the blessing, helpers and testimony of their victim. Accusing voices are speaking voices that always speak against and never in favor of their victim.

Accusing voices don't just accuse in vain. Accusing voicing operates on the ground of wickedness, and it becomes a legal reason for them to voice out. Accusing voices are invisible voices that cannot be visible seen, thou they can be heard.

And the LORD said unto Cain, Where [is] Abel thy brother? And he said, I know not: [Am] I my brother's keeper? And he said, What hast thou done? the voice of thy brother's blood crieth unto me from the ground. And now [art] thou cursed from the earth, which hath opened her mouth to receive thy brother's blood from thy hand; When thou tillest the ground, it shall not henceforth yield unto thee her strength; a fugitive and a vagabond shalt thou be in the earth. Gen 4:9-12.

God has defeated the accuser. Accusing voices has been existing since the days of Cain and Abel, the descendants of Adam and Eve. The blood of Abel was speaking against the life of Cain because Cain shed the blood of Abel.

Accusing voices are monitoring evil voices that used their voice of accusation to abort the expectation of their victim. Accusing spirit can operate from generation to generation, until they are silenced by the blood of Jesus. They can cause their victim to be denied of their benefits, promotion, breakthrough, favor, their right and their entitlement at a crucial time. This voices causes delay in expectation.

The goodnews

And I heard a loud voice saying in heaven, Now is come salvation, and strength, and the kingdom of our God, and the power of his Christ: for the accuser of our brethren is cast down, which accused them before our God day and night. Rev 12:10.

And they overcame him by the blood of the Lamb, and by the word of their testimony; and they loved not their lives unto the death. Rev 12:11.

[There is] therefore now no condemnation to them which are in Christ Jesus, who walk not after the flesh, but after the Spirit. For the law of the Spirit of life in Christ Jesus hath made me free from the law of sin and death. Rom 8:1-2.

Causes

1. It can be as a result of shedding the blood of innocent person.
2. It can be as a result of entering into covenant with demonic spirits.

3. It can be as a result of summoning of evil spirit to speak against someone.

Scriptural Confession

[Let] this [be] the reward of mine adversaries from the LORD, and of them that speak evil against my soul. Ps 109:20

Help me, O LORD my God: O save me according to thy mercy: That they may know that this [is] thy hand; [that] thou, LORD, hast done it. Let them curse, but bless thou: when they arise, let them be ashamed; but let thy servant rejoice. Let mine adversaries be clothed with shame, and let them cover themselves with their own confusion, as with a mantle. Ps 109:26-29.

No weapon that is formed against thee shall prosper; and every tongue [that] shall rise against thee in judgment thou shalt condemn. This [is] the heritage of the servants of the LORD, and their righteousness [is] of me, saith the LORD. Isa 54:17

Prayers

1. Oh Lord, thank you for this revelation in Jesus name.
2. Blood of Jesus, speak for me in Jesus name.
3. It is written, every tongue that rises against me in judgment shall be condemned in Jesus name. I therefore condemn evil voices speaking against my life and my breakthrough in Jesus name.
4. Every tongue that is decreeing evil against me, be destroyed by the consuming fire of the Holy Spirit in the name of Jesus.
5. Every accusing fingers, pointing against me, wither by fire in the name of Jesus.
6. Every ancestral evil blood speaking against my life and ware fare, I silence you with the blood of Jesus.

7. Every blood of anyone one that is speaking against my life, finance and business be silenced forever in the name of Jesus.

8. Every monitoring voices monitoring me and looking for opportunities to speak against me, be silence and destroyed in Jesus.

9. Every controlling voices speaking against and controlling good things away from me, be silenced and destroyed in the name of Jesus.

10. Every condemning voices sentencing my helpers and help into desolation be located with fire and silenced by the blood of Jesus.

11. Every strange personality behind evil voices and negative voices be destroyed by fire in the name of Jesus.

12. Every witchcraft voice, occultic voice, marine voice, serpentine power voice, demonic voice that focus on me to bring me down, be silenced and destroyed in the name of Jesus.

13. Any evil altar speaking against my financial fortune, business and well being, be consumed by the fire of the Holy Ghost in the name of Jesus.

14. Every ancestral powers and foundational strongman of darkness speaking against my ware fare, be silence and destroyed by fire in the name of Jesus.

15. Every voice of household wickedness speaking against my life, success, breakthrough, be destroyed in the name of Jesus.

16. Every voice of my grandparent and parent that may be speaking negatively against my life, business, finance etc, be silenced by the blood of Jesus in the name of Jesus.

17. Any legal accusation that permit the operation of evil and negative voices against my life and ware fare be nullified by the blood of Jesus.

18. I released myself from every negative voice in the name of Jesus.

19. I release my business, organization, help and helpers, blessings from every evil voice in the name of Jesus.

20. I command every weeping voices to be silenced in the name of Jesus.

21. I command every agonizing voices to be silenced in the name of Jesus.

22. I command every disturbing voices to be silenced in the name of Jesus.

23. I command every manipulating voices to be silenced in the name of Jesus.

24. I command every hindering voices to be silenced in the name of Jesus.

25. I command every terrifying evil voices to be silenced in the name of Jesus.

26. I command every ill voice to be silenced in the name of Jesus.

27. I command every forces, agents, demons, personality behind any evil and negative voices and cry to depart from me by fire in the mighty name of Jesus.

28. I shut every door to strange voices forever in the name of Jesus.

29. Thank you Jesus for answered prayer in Jesus name.

17

Destroying The Operation Of Evil Hands

Their enemies also oppressed them, and they were brought into subjection under their hand. Ps 106:42

There are different kinds of hands. As we have good hands, we have evil hands. Evil hands stand for all the opposite of what a good hand stands for. Evil hand is an invisible hand of the enemy that is used in oppressing their victim and putting them in bondage and subjection to their evil will.

Evil hands exist. Evil hands are actually spiritual hands of darkness that operate by stealing, hijacking, stopping and diverting the riches and wealth of people. When the benefits of people are under the operation of evil hands, that hand will deny them of their benefits. Evil hands oppress, evil hands hide good things, evil hands afflict, evil hands steals.

Evil hand is evil. Anything an evil hand is laid upon will be destroyed. Evil hands labor to frustrate effort of his victim. Evil hand cages people and their glory.

Evil hand will hold good thing down. Anything evil hand is laid upon will not succeed. Evil hand can be stretched from any quarters. It can be the hand of witchcraft agent, polluting and planting evil in people's life, occultic hand pointing itself against good thing to destroy the value of such thing, or satanic hand that holds down people and keep them in captivity.

Some Of The Operations Of Evil Hands

1. Evil hands steals people's benefits
2. Evil hands stop the flow of money.
3. Evil hands manipulate destinies.
4. Evil hands stagnate.
5. Evil hands oppress people physically and spiritually
6. An evil hand makes people to labor in vain.
7. Evil hands cause oppression.

How To Deal With Evil Hands

1. Identify the pattern of its operation.
2. Engage the fire of God to consume them: Jer. 5:15, Ps; 97:3.
3. Pray violently against their operation.

Scriptural confession

For the rod of the wicked shall not rest upon the lot of the righteous; lest the righteous put forth their hands unto iniquity. Ps 125:3

Keep me, O LORD, from the hands of the wicked; preserve me from the violent man; who have purposed to overthrow my goings. Ps 140:4

Send thine hand from above; rid me, and deliver me out of great waters, from the hand of strange children; Whose mouth speaketh vanity, and their right hand [is] a right hand of falsehood. Ps 144:7-8

Break thou the arm of the wicked and the evil [man]: seek out his wickedness [till] thou find none. Ps 10:15

Prayers

1. Any evil hand engineering poverty in my life, wither by fire in the name of Jesus.
2. Any occultic hands controlling the affairs of my finance be cut off by the authority in the name of Jesus.
3. Any hand stealing my money, be cut off by the sword of fire in the name of Jesus.
4. Any evil hands diverting my blessing wither in the name of Jesus.
5. Any evil hand that is holding down good things in my life and business, lose your hold and wither in the name of Jesus.
6. I command every evil hand in charge of my blessings, benefits and money to be cut off by the authority in the name of Jesus.
7. Every ancestral evil hands, that is scattering as I am gathering, be cut off in Jesus name.
8. Holy Ghost fire, expose all evil hands troubling the affairs of my hands and consume them to ashes in the name of Jesus.
9. My wealth in the hand of darkness, be released by fire in the name of Jesus.
10. I recover my wealth, riches, money in any evil hands in Jesus name.
11. Any hand that has illegally withheld my money, I command fire upon that hand and I command such hand to release my withheld benefits in the name of Jesus.
12. Every ruling hands that has been joined together to fight me, scatter in the name of Jesus.

13. I command the release of my benefits from every where it is being withheld in Jesus name.

14. Oh Lord, by your hands of fire deliver me and my glory from the hands of the wicked in the name of Jesus.

15. Any evil hands that wants to kill be, wither by fire in the name of Jesus.

16. I receive victory over evil hands in the name of Jesus.

18

Breaking The Network Of Darkness

[Though] hand [join] in hand, the wicked shall not be unpunished: but the seed of the righteous shall be delivered. Prov. 11:21

Network of darkness is an interconnectivity of the powers of darkness to fight against an individual, family or an organization. It is the gathering of more than one demonic agent. It is the gathering of various demonic agents against someone. It is a combination of force and power to destroy and fight against their victim.

When demonic agents network together, it is so that they can overcome their victim at all cost. Satanic network is the conjunction or coming together of dark powers in order to destroy destinies, hinder progress and cause frustration. But see what the bible say.

Behold, they shall surely gather together, [but] not by me: whosoever shall gather together against thee shall fall for thy sake. Isa 54:15

The bible says, they shall surely gather. It means, this is not the first time they are gathering, it also means expect them to gather and network, but they shall fall at your feet in prayer. When they network and gather against you, It is to make life difficult for you.

Why evil network?

1. They network so that they can monitor your activities and hinder it.
2. They network so that it will be hard for their victims to escape from their raider and evil plan.
3. They network so that if you escape one, you will not escape another.
4. They network to make life difficult for their victim.
5. They network so that they can block all avenue good things can locate their victim.
6. They network to keep their victim in perpetual bondage and trauma.
7. They network so that anywhere their victim relocate to, he will meet them there and face the same difficulties they place upon him.

Keys To Your Freedom

1. Knowledge of truth:

Ye shall know the truth and the truth shall set you free. John 8:32 What is the truth? *Thy word is truth. John 17:17.* Jesus is truth. 14:6. the word of God is truth. What is the word? Jesus is the word. Jesus is truth. And the bible says, if the son shall make you free you shall be free indeed. John 8:36. The truth is that Jesus has set you free from the operation of the powers of darkness. You must confess this truth in prayers. No power of darkness has any right to frustrate you in any way again.

2. Violent and relentless prayers:

And from the days of John the Baptist until now the kingdom of heaven suffereth violence, and the violent take it by force. Matt 11:12

There is necessity for aggressive and violent prayer. If you are not violent with your enemies, they will refuse to let you go. Prayer of violent and ceaseless prayer is the key to freedom. Pray like you are not going to stop, pray like everything depends on it.

Scriptural confession:
Read whole of Psalm 2.

Associate yourselves, O ye people, and ye shall be broken in pieces; and give ear, all ye of far countries: gird yourselves, and ye shall be broken in pieces; gird yourselves, and ye shall be broken in pieces. Take counsel together, and it shall come to nought; speak the word, and it shall not stand: for God [is] with us. Isa 8:9, 10

Deliver me, O LORD, from mine enemies: I flee unto thee to hide me. Ps 143:9

Behold, they shall surely gather together, [but] not by me: whosoever shall gather together against thee shall fall for thy sake. Isa 54:15

[Though] hand [join] in hand, the wicked shall not be unpunished: but the seed of the righteous shall be delivered. Prov 11:21

Prayers
1. Oh Lord, arise and fight for me in the name of Jesus.
2. Oh Lord, show me great mercy in the name of Jesus.
3. Oh Lord, in your mercy cut off all my enemies in the name of Jesus.
4. I release warrior angel against all my adversaries in the name of Jesus.
5. Any where they are gathering against my doing well in life, Oh Lord my father scatter them in Jesus name.

6. Every evil network and activities against my life break away in the name of Jesus.

7. Every evil decision, conclusion and judgment against me, be cancelled by the blood of Jesus.

8. Oh Lord, expose all the workers of iniquity of my life in the name of Jesus.

9. Every evil hand that is joined together against me, break off and scatter in the name of Jesus.

10. Every seat of the enemy against me be vacant in the name of Jesus.

11. Any evil altar they gather and network against me scatter by fire in the name of Jesus.

12. Anything in nature that has been commanded to work against my success and prosperity, disconnect and fail in the name of Jesus.

13. Every satanic power behind evil network and operation in my life, be exposed and defeated in the name of Jesus.

14. Oh Lord, deliver me permanently from evil network in the name of Jesus.

15. Any people gather against my prosperity and well being, disagree and scatter in the name of Jesus.

19

Commanding Anointing for Financial Favor

Thou preparest a table before me in the presence of mine enemies: thou anointest my head with oil; my cup runneth over. Ps 23:5

God is always at work releasing favor upon his people. However, you are the one that will command the favor of God upon you. When favor is commanded into your life and business, it will bring all the desirable expectation of your heart. It takes favor to be enriched. To command in order word is to speak by authority in calling forth the favor of God to rest upon you and all that pertains to you, or to do a good deed that will qualify you for the automatic release of favor.

God is a distributor of favor. If He decides to favor you with financial favor, money will flow into your hand and business so easily. Divine favor of God is not a function of your hard-work, but of God's mercy.

Favor is real in God. Favor is the virtue from God that adds color to what you are doing. Favor attract surplus of financial fortune. Nothing grows from small to multitude without the divine favor of God. Favor is a way of God blessing a man for his own sake. When it was time for God to lift Joseph, God unleash the wonder of favor.

And he left all that he had in Joseph's hand; and he knew not ought he had, save the bread which he did eat. And Joseph was [a] goodly [person], and well favoured. Gen 39:6

But the LORD was with Joseph, and shewed him mercy, and gave him favour in the sight of the keeper of the prison. Gen 39:21

Everywhere Joseph turns to; the favor of God speaks upon his life. The favor of God followed Joseph from his father's house, to the pit, and to the prison even till he became a prime minister in Egypt and became very blessed and great.

When God releases financial favor upon you, everywhere you turn, you will be attracting financial fortune as cheaply as possible, but when favor is lacking, all the money you earn will be through hard labor.

Something about this favor is that it is God that gives this favor. He gave the Israelite favor when they were leaving Egypt.

And I will give this people favour in the sight of the Egyptians: and it shall come to pass, that, when ye go, ye shall not go empty: Exod 3:21.

When the Lord gave the Israelite favor before their enemies, it was their enemies that supplied them provision for their journey.

And the LORD gave the people favour in the sight of the Egyptians, so that they lent unto them [such things as they required]. And they spoiled the Egyptians. Exod. 12:36.

They left with so much silver and gold and clothing that the Egyptians emptied out all their goods to them. Through the favor of God, the Israelite became very wealthy.

Favor brings multiplication; continuous operation of favor brings continuous multiplication and increase. Favor aid in the prosperity and expansion of any thriving venture. The apostles who went about preaching about Jesus and the kingdom of God enjoyed uncommon favor of God and God increased the church and her finance as well.

Praising God, and having favour with all the people. And the Lord added to the church daily such as should be saved. Acts 2:47.

If you must breakthrough to the realm of financial rest, it requires the working operation of continuous favor of God in your life. And you can receive this favor by demand. If there is a demand, there will be a supply.

How To Be Qualified For Divine Favor

1. Accept Jesus into your life. Prov. 8:35.
   For whoso findeth me findeth life, and shall obtain favour of the LORD. Prov 8:35.

2. Be a good man…Prov. 12:2
   A good [man] obtaineth favour of the LORD: but a man of wicked devices will he condemn.

3. Find yourself a good wife and get married legally. Prov. 18:22
   [Whoso] findeth a wife findeth a good [thing], and obtaineth favour of the LORD.

4. Have good understanding of God and life. Prov. 13:15

Good understanding giveth favour: but the way of transgressors [is] hard.

5. Ask for the favor of God. Ps. 5:12
    For thou, LORD, wilt bless the righteous; with favour wilt thou compass him as [with] a shield.

Scriptures

And whatsoever ye shall ask in my name, that will I do, that the Father may be glorified in the Son.
If ye shall ask any thing in my name, I will do [it]. John 14:13-14.

For thou, LORD, wilt bless the righteous; with favour wilt thou compass him as [with] a shield. Ps 5:12

For thou [art] the glory of their strength: and in thy favour our horn shall be exalted. Ps 89:17

Remember me, O LORD, with the favour [that thou bearest unto] thy people: O visit me with thy salvation; Ps 106:4

I intreated thy favour with [my] whole heart: be merciful unto me according to thy word. Ps 119:58

Prayers

1. Oh Lord, show me your favor in Jesus name.
2. Oh Lord, release upon me the anointing of financial favor in the name of Jesus.
3. Power of favor, possess me in Jesus name.
4. Emblem of favor stamp upon me in the name of Jesus.
5. Angel of financial favor appear and locate me for financial breakthrough in Jesus name.

6. Atmosphere of favor, envelop me in the name of Jesus.

7. Wind of financial favor flow into my life in the name of
    Jesus.

20

Possessing the Power to Renewing Your Mind

For as he thinketh in his heart, so [is] he: Eat and drink, saith he to thee; but his heart [is] not with thee. Prov. 23:7.

As a man thinks in his heart, so is he. Your mind is the control room of your destiny. Your mind determines what you become. It is the seat of your outcome. You can never be better than what you think. You must choose your thought careful. Your thought determines your take.

Poverty is first a mindset before it is a life set. What you conceive in your mind is what you will flow into your life. Some people who never thought of becoming great, rich, wealthy cannot be. As a man think, so he is. If you don't think right, things cannot go right for you. Right thought will produce right word, right words will produce right result.

Say ye to the righteous, that [it shall be] well [with him]: for they shall eat the fruit of their doings. Isa 3:10

God is careful of his words. His word is a product of his thought. And his words once declared, cannot be reversed. And so he knows the power of words and thoughts us so. What you don't see in your mind you can't receive in your hands. Your mind has to be transformed to a rich mindset.

There is no wealth principle that works without the right mindset. Right mindset will give birth to right attitude. Right attitude will result in a great outcome. Your mind is your first source of wealth. If you subject your mind to poor thinking, you will become poor, if you subject your mind to greatness, you will be great. Your real thought is revealed in what you say when you are going through hard times. Be cautious. Begin to reject what you don't want. Your mind can launch you into the realm of prosperity or valley of poverty. You have a choice to adjust and refill your mind with words of life.

And be not conformed to this world: but be ye transformed by the renewing of your mind, that ye may prove what [is] that good, and acceptable, and perfect, will of God. Rom 12:2

Let your mind be renewed. Stop all your negative believe and thought. Stop all your negative dogmas and fate. A renewed mind can change any fate. A renewed mind is a convinced mind. A mind that has been made up to stand on the word of faith, a renewed mind is an unlimited mind. A mind that believe all things are possible.

Your Thought Can Make You Rich

Napoleon Hills wrote a book and titled it, *think and grow rich*. Your thought can make you rich. Riches come from the mind. Riches is not anywhere, it is in the mind. When your mind has been fully persuaded and settled for riches then you have opened the door to attract wealth. When you mind changes, wealth will change hands. Wealth will come navigating towards you.

How To Renew Your Mind

1. Read life changing books
2. Read the word of God to build your faith

3. Pray against fear, doubt, low self esteem and satanic manipulation

Scriptural Confession

Thou shalt also decree a thing, and it shall be established unto thee: and the light shall shine upon thy ways. When [men] are cast down, then thou shalt say, [There is] lifting up; and he shall save the humble person. Job 22:28-29

Prayers

1. I cast out fear and doubt in my life in the name of Jesus.
2. I sanitize my heart and cast out every stranger of low self esteem in Jesus name.
3. I uproot every seed of poverty rooted in my heart in the name of Jesus.
4. Every wrong motive and believe I have against prosperity and success; I renounce and reject you in the name of Jesus.
5. My mind receives divine transformation in the name of Jesus.
6. My life receives divine transformation in Jesus name.

21

Heavens Of My Financial Fortune, Open

Oh that thou wouldest rend the heavens, that thou wouldest come down, that the mountains might flow down at thy presence, Isa 64:1

Many people operate under closed heaven. When the heaven is closed against a person, the person will be frustrated because the dimension of hardship in his life will be grade one hardship. While on the other hand, when the heavens open over a person, he will experience continuous release of blessing over his life and over all he is doing.

Jesus said, no one can receive anything except it is given to him from above. James concluded, every *good gift and every perfect gift is from above, and cometh down from the Father of lights, with whom is no variableness, neither shadow of turning. Jas 1:17*

All the gift released from above answers to open heaven. When a man's heaven is opened he will enjoy sweatless supply of good things from God. Everything a man possesses comes from above, you may say but money is here on earth, how come it comes from above. Everything answers to heavens release.

Jesus answered, Thou couldest have no power [at all] against me, except it were given thee from above: therefore he that delivered me unto thee hath the greater sin. John 19:11

Jesus was addressing Pilate the governor here, which implies that a leader's authority and power comes from above. The day heaven closes over that man; his authority will cease to function.

To enjoy uncommon financial fortune you need to tap into the operation of open heaven.

Open heaven is a proof that God is in support of what you are doing, and He is behind your prosperity.

The LORD shall open unto thee his good treasure, **the heaven to give the rain unto thy land** *in his season, and to bless all the work of thine hand: and thou shalt lend unto many nations, and thou shalt not borrow.*
Deut 28:12

The scripture above is saying, God will command the heaven to give the rain unto your business or whatever you are doing that will fetch you money. It is the heaven that releases upon the earth, from what the earth has also release into heaven. Every sacrifice and good deed you do here goes up as sweet smelling savor for release of God's blessing from above.

In these however, you must understand that there are different dimension of open heavens. The heaven we are commanding to open is the heavens of financial fortune. When the heavens open, riches are inevitable in that business.

This section is for you, you are responsible for your open heavens. If you heart is fully connected, the heaven can open for you immediately. When the heavens open you will see the hand of God upon your life immediately, and there will visible manifestation of divine financial turnaround.

Do everything sacrificially, prayerfully, and in tithing to ensure your heavens open. This may be what your destiny has been waiting for to launch you into the realm of your own fortune.

When your heavens open, God will release his good treasures of fortune to bless you. Your heavens shall open this season in Jesus name.

People Who Experienced Open Heavens In The Bible

1. Ezekiel experienced open heavens, and he heard the voice of God that liberated him from captivity. Ezekiel 1:1,3
2. Elijah experienced open heavens and rain came down from heaven upon Israel and famine of three and half years ended. 1Kings 18:41-46
3. Jesus experienced open heavens when he was undergoing baptism, and God confirmed him as His beloveth son. Matthew 3:16-17
4. Stephens experienced open heaven and he saw Jesus at the right hand of God. Act 7:56.
5. Peter experienced open heaven where he was given a mandate to save the household of Cornelius. Act 10:9-15.

What are the things you can do to provoke open heaven
1. Accept Jesus into your life.
2. Provoke heaven with praise.
3. Provoke heaven with your sacrificial seed offering
4. Pray violent as led by the Holy Spirit.

Benefits of Open heaven
✓ When the heavens opened there will be divine visitation.
✓ When the heavens opened there will be divine accreditation.
✓ When the heavens opened there will be divine encounter.

- ✓ When the heavens opened there will be divine communication.
- ✓ When the heavens open there will be divine favor.
- ✓ When the heavens open thee will be divine touch.

Scriptural confession:

Give ear, O ye heavens, and I will speak; and hear, O earth, the words of my mouth. Deut 32:1.

The LORD shall open unto thee his good treasure, the heaven to give the rain unto thy land in his season, and to bless all the work of thine hand: and thou shalt lend unto many nations, and thou shalt not borrow. Deut 28:12

Prayers

Start with praise and worship before you start the prayer;

1. Oh Lord, I thank you because of your faithfulness and mercy in Jesus name.
2. In the name of Jesus, heaven of mercy open over me.
3. In the name of Jesus, heaven of favor open over me.
4. Oh Lord, rend the heaven opens and release all my benefits in the name of Jesus.
5. Heaven of my financial breakthrough open by fire in the name of Jesus.
6. Every obstacles and barrier against my open heaven be removed by fire in the name of Jesus.
7. Heaven of my financial helpers open in the mighty name of Jesus.
8. Oh Lord, open unto me the heavens of blessing that will launch me into indefinite prosperity in Jesus name.
9. Oh Lord, open my eyes to experience my open heaven in the name of Jesus.

10. My blessing from above, be released and locate me in the name of Jesus.

11. My fortune from above, be released and locate me in the name of Jesus.

12. My help from above, be released and locate me in the name of Jesus.

13. My riches from above, be released and locate me in the name of Jesus.

14. Thank you for answered prayer in Jesus name.

22

Open My Eyes To My Source Of Prosperity

And God opened her eyes, and she saw a well of water; and she went, and filled the bottle with water, and gave the lad drink. Gen 21:19.

God is an eye opener. When he wants to bless you, he opens your eyes to an opportunity that will change your life, or opens the eyes of someone to believe in you and recommend an opportunity to you. All that is important is for your eyes to be opened. Until your eyes are opened, you cannot see the opportunity that will make you rich.

And God opened her eyes, and she saw a well of water...
Hagar was left without water, the water she carried on her journey was finished, and she was dying of thirst with her little lad. Both of them were near death, as the lad was crying, God spoke to Hagar and opened her eyes to see a well of water beside her. That was all they needed to survive drought.

There is an opportunity around everyone that can bring in riches. Opportunity abounds around you, though not all opportunity will prosper you but the one God prepares for you to prosper you. Why God must open your eyes is so that you can differentiate between the opportunity meant for your prosperity and the one that can bring you bankruptcy. When you see, you will be able to avoid the one that will make you bankrupt and tap into the one that will usher in your prosperity.

God needs to open your eyes because not all opportunities are genuine. Not all opportunity is meant for you. Not all opportunity will bring you fulfillment of dreams.

Why your eyes must be opened

- ✓ When your eyes are opened, you will have clear understanding of what is happening.
- ✓ When your eyes are opened you will see clear picture of what is obtainable for you
- ✓ When your eyes are opened you will see the path to follow.
- ✓ When your eyes are opened you will escape every trap of poverty.
- ✓ When your eyes are opened it open your life to transformation.
- ✓ When your eyes are opened it will put an end to all your questions and worries.
- ✓ When your eyes are opened you will be connected to right opportunities.
- ✓ When your eyes are opened you will discover what is meant for you and what is not meant for you.
- ✓ When your eyes are opened you will be satisfied with good things.

Scriptural confession

Open thou mine eyes, that I may behold wondrous things out of thy law. Ps 119:18

The LORD openeth [the eyes of] the blind: the LORD raiseth them that are bowed down: the LORD loveth the righteous: Ps 146:8

Call unto me, and I will answer thee, and shew thee great and mighty things, which thou knowest not. Jer. 33:3

Prayers:

1. Oh Lord, open my eyes to what to do next in Jesus name.
2. Oh Lord, open my eyes to the opportunity you have prepared for me.
3. Oh Lord, open my eyes to the path I should follow in Jesus name.
4. Oh Lord, open my eyes and save me from tragedies in Jesus name.
5. Open my eyes to my source of prosperity in life in Jesus name.

23
Divine Connection To Prosperity Helpers

Therefore thy gates shall be open continually; they shall not be shut day nor night; that [men] may bring unto thee the forces of the Gentiles, and [that] their kings [may be] brought. Isa 60:11

Divine connection is a connection orchestrated by God to meet one's destiny's helpers and financial helpers. To every money that comes your way and will come your way, there is need for a link. This link is what is called divine connection. Divine connection however is when God establish a divine link that will bridge the gap between you and your helpers. God has the power to bring in your helper to you without struggle. Your prosperity helpers could be your business partners, your sponsors, or even a friend. Prosperity helpers are those who contribute to your prosperity in one way or the other. They will do whatever it takes to support you from moving from your financial valley to your financial mountain. Helper means getting a divine assistance that you need for your divine turn around which you as individual cannot render for yourself.

Helper of prosperity is those who create that opportunity that you need to make a positive difference in your life. Helpers will not leave you the way they met you, they will affect your life positively and turn your fortune around.

People in search of prosperity are much, but those who want to help are few. Your helper may not really be a multi millionaire, but someone with the tool, information, stuff you need to launch you into your own financial fortune.

Divine connection is a way of God connecting you to those who will help you to achieve your dreams as your dream will help others to fulfill their own purpose. Divine connection is the bridge between you and your helpers. When God decide to connect you to a helper, he will also make the helpers to be willing to help in such a way that the help will meet the higher expectation of launching you into your prosperity.

Who you know does not matter, like who God connect you to. You can know wealthy people, captains of industry, successful tycoon who are not willing to make a difference in your life, but when God is involved, He will raise you help from men that will make your achieve all your dreams without sweat and pleading. God factor is the major factor in the pathway to prosperity and riches in this regard. When God is removed from the equation, struggle and disappointment will be inevitable. However, whatever God is involved fully in will experience a major divine turn around that will be visible to men.

Let the source of your divine connection be influenced by God and not by eye service and selling out your integrity. When God connect you, he will also honor you before your helpers. When you make the connection yourself, he may not have much regard. And you will likely be their boy.

Keys To Divine Connection
1. Be connected to Christ himself. John 15:5
2. Be rightly position. Ps. 37:23
3. Pray always. Luke 18:1
4. Trust God for divine connection. Prov. 3:5
5. Sow seed for divine connection. Eccl. 11:6.

Scriptural confession:

Thou shalt arise, [and] have mercy upon Zion: for the time to favour her, yea, the set time, is come. Ps 102:13

Hear me when I call, O God of my righteousness: thou hast enlarged me [when I was] in distress; have mercy upon me, and hear my prayer. Ps 4:1

Prayers

1. Oh Lord, arise in your favor towards me my Lord and My God in Jesus name.
2. Oh Lord, open the door of divine connection for me in Jesus name.
3. Oh Lord, connect me to my prosperity helpers in Jesus name.
4. Oh Lord, loose me from any spot I am tied in Jesus name.
5. Oh Lord my father, move me to where I am needed in Jesus name.
6. Oh Lord, send down your rain of mercy upon my life in Jesus name.
7. Oh Lord, for divine connection to every rightful people my life needed come upon me in the name of Jesus.

24
Mantle Of Prosperity, Fall On Me

And Elijah took his mantle, and wrapped [it] together, and smote the waters, and they were divided hither and thither, so that they two went over on dry ground. 2Kgs 2:8

Mantle is the enabling power of God to prosper financially. Mantle is not visible. It is the spiritual context of prosperity. Mantle of prosperity is the key of prosperity in the hand of God to the hand of man.

Power is the ability to do work. Ability means the appropriate effort needed to achieve something. It is not everyone that has the ability needed to make money. Idea is not enough to make money, connection is not enough to make money, effort is not enough to make money, it is the power from above that makes the difference. The success factor of financial breakthrough is the divine power involved to make the wealth available.

It takes the mantle of prosperity to command uncommon financial outcome. A good case study is the encounter of Elisha with the mantle of Elijah. When the mantle fell upon Elisha, the same result the mantle generated in the hands of Elijah, it generated it in the hands of Elisha.

And he took the mantle of Elijah that fell from him, and smote the waters, and said, Where [is] the LORD God of Elijah? and when he also had smitten the waters, they parted hither and thither: and Elisha went over. 2Kgs 2:14

The mantle in this case is the mantle of signs and wonders. Prophetic assignment of Elisha would not be potent without this mantle. The mantle of prosperity is needed to end financial frustration.

Mantle is like an unction that is released from someone who carries the unction to someone who needs it. One of the cheapest way to get the mantle is to locate the mantle carrier and contact the grace for the mantle. This mantle of prosperity swallows every trace of poverty in your life. It consumes and destroy every stubborn yoke of poverty and lack and liberate you into your future of endless financial fortune. this mantle will turn a pauper to prosper beyond expectation.

How to locate the mantle carrier

1. A man of God with the mantle for prosperity.
2. A man of God that God leads you to sow into their lives to enhance your prosperity.
3. A place of worship that carries the grace for prosperity.
4. Someone who carries the grace through which others under them prospers supernaturally.

Factors prosperity responds to:

1. **Willingness to prosper: Isaiah 1:19**
   Willingness is the personal motivation and the driving force to attain to financial prosperity. If you are not willing, you will not be determined.

2. **Obedience to God: Job 36:11**

If they obey and serve [him], they shall spend their days in prosperity, and their years in pleasures. Job 36:11.

Obedience is the ability to learn, know, observe and do what God has commanded you to do in order to get what God has prepared as promised.

3. **Sowing without ceasing:**

Seeing is a principle that works in giving birth to harvest. Sowing is not something that is done once. It is deliberate and continuous. Sowing must be done consciously with the understanding that is firm enough to keep the sowing regular regardless

4. **Ability to serve God:**

If you obey and serve him you will spend your days in prosperity. Serving God is part of what is required to get prosperity. Serving God is a command. Serving God makes God who is the giver of fortune to delight in favoring you with his fortune.

5. **Hard work: Ecc. 9:10**

whatsoever thy hand findeth to do, do [it] with thy might; for [there is] no work, nor device, nor knowledge, nor wisdom, in the grave, whither thou goest.

Anything your hands find to do, do it with all your might says the word of God. Money does not fall from heaven. When a man is diligent in his work with the favor of God upon his work, he will be on his way to financial fortune.

6. **Ability to multiply money:** Prov. 21:20

[There is] treasure to be desired and oil in the dwelling of the wise; but a foolish man spendeth it up.

Money grows in the hand of the man that knows how to invest it and money goes in the hand of those who knows how to spend it. Money multiplication strategy is a skill needed to help you to increase your cash flow.

Scriptural declaration
Save now, I beseech thee, O LORD: O LORD, I beseech thee, send now prosperity. Ps 118:25

Prayers
1. Oh Lord, release into my hands the mantle of prosperity in Jesus name.
2. Every door of prosperity that is shut against me be open in the name of Jesus.
3. The uncommon grace to succeed and prosper financially fall upon me in Jesus name.
4. Oh Ye anointing of prosperity fall upon me in the name of Jesus.

25

Prayers For Ideas For Streams Of Income

But [there is] a spirit in man: and the inspiration of the Almighty giveth them understanding. Job 32:8

Idea they say rules the world. Idea is a divine inspiration of God in a man. Idea is not what you assume it is what God inspires in you. Idea is given to change destiny. When a seed of ideas grows in your hand, it will put an end to your poverty and bring prosperity. Ideas are the magnet of prosperity. When divine ideas come inside of you, it will turn you to another man.

Ideas make you happy and confidence. It gives you hope of a brighter future and make you believe in the certainty of tomorrow. It takes idea to secure the future. One idea is enough to change your life. Idea is not ambition, idea is inspiration. Inspiration is stirring of your spirit man to receive the idea gift of destiny. Idea is the key to unlocking wealth.

When God inspires idea in you, it is a sign that God wants to change your life from what it used to be to the best it can be. Idea makes life beautiful. As you will be praying for divine inspiration and release of idea, you must be hopeful and expectant. Idea is the guide to limelight.

It is God that inspires idea. Whatever God inspires, he will protect it, preserve it, provide for it, pronounce it and promote it. You need more than one streams of income to have more than enough financial flow into your life.

And so the entrance of an idea in a man's life, makes a colorless life to become colorful.

Scriptural confession:
And thine ears shall hear a word behind thee, saying, This [is] the way, walk ye in it, when ye turn to the right hand, and when ye turn to the left. Isa 30:21

And whatsoever ye shall ask in my name, that will I do, that the Father may be glorified in the Son.
If ye shall ask any thing in my name, I will do [it]. John 14:13-14

Prayers
1. Oh Lord, hear my voice and bless me today in Jesus name.
2. Oh Lord, open doors for ideas and streams of income in my life in Jesus name.
3. Oh Lord, release a divine idea unto me that will change the course of my life forever in the name of Jesus.
4. Every idea killers in my life, be arrested din the mighty name of Jesus.
5. Any power assigned to terminate my idea, be terminated in Jesus name.
6. Angels of idea, visit me and release the idea my life has been waiting for in the name of Jesus.
7. Oh Lord, finance my ideas in Jesus name.
8. Oh Lord, raise me people that will sponsor this ideas in Jesus name.
9. Power of God to succeed with this idea fall on me in Jesus name.

10. Oh Lord, promote this idea all over the world in the name of Jesus.

11. Thank you Lord for answered prayers.

26

Breaking The Yoke Of Repeated Failure

For it shall come to pass in that day, saith the LORD of hosts, [that] I will break his yoke from off thy neck, and will burst thy bonds, and strangers shall no more serve themselves of him: Jer 30:8

Failure in life has a tendency of keeping a man on the ground. An unsuccessful man cannot boast of a desirable financial purse. Many people gives up when their failure rate is unbearable, as a matter of fact, failure comes as a surprise to so many people.

Failure can be so painful, It is an hope dasher. However relevant knowledge of this topic has to be known so that you can overcome it maximally. If you can truly know how to bypass failure, you will consider other areas of your life encouraging.

What Is Failure?

Failure is an art of disappointment that arises as a result of making relevant effort. It means to make effort and not succeed as expected, to be defeated after so much plans and preparation. Failure can be a waste of time and resources. It also means unexplainable inability to reach your goal.

Failure is not final. God has not design any one to be a failure. The law of God is created to subdue the power of failure. Failure hinders a man from promotion. It keeps a person in the same spot, state. Failure at some level can still be overlooked to move on, but failure at other failure brings total discouragement and disappointment.

Because you made several effort and never succeeded does not actually means that you should give in and quit. Failure challenges you to better prepare for your pursuit. The race of success is surrounding with the balloon of failure, failure is a better builder of men. Men who have experience failures in life are stronger, more experience on the subject of success. Failure is cause by some road blocks, which you must know and address.

Overcoming the power of failure, from the subject, failure can sometimes be so powerful to limit you at some point. But you will need to rise above the power of failure to succeed. You have tried, and given it all it takes in that venture, but yet, you still never got to the top. The fact is that you have not been empower to overcome the power of failure. When one power is stronger than the other, one has to subdue the other. If the power of failure is stronger than the power of will, it may end up defeated as usual.

You must overcome the stronghold of failure over your life if you want to become what you dream to be, if you want to get to your promise land. Failure can keep a man in the valley of poverty.

Causes Of Failure

1. Lack of knowledge: Hos. 4:6
2. Lack of divine direction. Prov. 14:12
3. Lack of vision. Prov. 29:18
4. Lack of skill. Daniel 1:17
5. Lack of favor: Deut. 28:50
6. Lack of help and helper. John 5:7
7. Lack of resources.
8. Lack of zeal and determination
9. Lack of opportunities.

10. Laziness. Prov. 6:9-11

11. Procrastination. Prov.12:27

12. Wrong association. Prov. 13:20

13. Prayerlessness. Matt. 26:36-40

14. Disobedience to the instruction of God. Job 36:12

15. Wrong attitude to life. Gal. 5:15

16. Inability to keep secret. Prov. 11:13

17. Addiction. Prov. 21:26

18. Satanic hindrance: 1thes. 2:18

19. Lack of capacity.

20. Non challant attitude

21. Dreams of failure

22. Curse of failure

23. Playfulness:

Level of failures

1. Normal failure:

Normal failure is common; it is the failure that comes as a result of ignorance in some areas. Normal failure requires putting in more effort, and trying all you could to get the result. If you press more, and try again you will reach your goal.

2. Chronic failure

Chronic failure is the degree of failure that is repeating itself. It is an harden failure type. Despite skills, input, effort, it ends in failure. Chronic failure is a total time waster. Many people that are product of chronic failure, gives up in life, or commit suicide. All their effort to make something work, does not yield any form of result. They have tried all they could, strategies, plan and taken all manner of steps, advice and counsel, yet they ended up not succeeding. It is actually frustrating. This kind of failure is also called abnormal failure, it is demonic in nature, and it requires fasting and prayer to break the yoke of this kind of failure.

3. Hereditary failure:

It is a failure that is inherited. This is failure in the bloodline. The father failed in that area and the children are also failing in that area. It is the kind of failure that operates in the bloodline of those people. You must understand, this kind of failure can be as a result of curse, covenant or violating certain agreement. Hereditary failure is a failure symptom that is plaguing every member of a failure. It is uniform in nature.

Areas of life where failure manifest

1. Spiritual failure
2. Marital failure
3. Financial failure
4. Ministerial failure
5. Career and business failure
6. Health failure
7. Character failure

How To Overcome failure

1. Discover the causes of your failure.
2. Be determined to succeed.
3. Acquire relevant skill and knowledge.
4. Put in fasting and prayer.
5. Operate on scriptural principles.

Prayers

1. Oh Lord my father, liberate me from every operation of unknown causes of failure in Jesus.
2. Ancestral yoke of failure in my life be destroyed in Jesus name.
3. Ancestral curse of failure be nullified in the name of Jesus
4. Every pronouncement of failure in my life be cancelled in the name of Jesus.
5. Every decrees and spells of failure in my life, be cancelled by the blood of Jesus.
6. Every satanic forces of failure in my life, be destroyed in Jesus.
7. Every repeated yoke of failure in my life, break by fire in the name of Jesus.
8. Any power arresting my progress, release it and die in Jesus name.
9. Every power behind failure in my, die in the name of Jesus.
10. Every obstruction on my way of success be removed in Jesus name.
11. Every stronghold of failure in my foundation, collapse and perish in the name of Jesus.
12. Power of God to succeed fall on me in Jesus name.
13. Power of God to make it fall on me in the name of Jesus name.

27

My Financial Glory, Manifest

[There is] one glory of the sun, and another glory of the moon, and another glory of the stars: for [one] star differeth from [another] star in glory. 1Cor 15:41

Everything God create has it glory. A man is the glory of God's work. The glory is the key to the fruitfulness. Glory allows the man to proof is worth. When the glory is missing, there cannot be any form of manifestation. It is the manifestation of glory that brings forth success and breakthrough. Glory is God's divine deposit in you that will showcase you to the world.

Financial glory is the glory of your finance. When your finance is manifesting glory, whatever you lay hand on will be generating great income. Glory is a success activator. The best of everything comes out when the glory manifest.

It takes glory to manifest greatness. When the glory is manifesting, it will be bringing forth in multiplication and increase. Your financial glory must manifest if you want to enjoy financial fortune.

This beginning of miracles did Jesus in Cana of Galilee, and manifested forth his glory; and his disciples believed on him. John 2:11

There are different kinds of glory. The glory of destiny fulfillment is different from the glory of marriage, and that of marriage is different from the glory of finance. If one glory is manifesting and financial glory is not manifesting. You will be doing well in that arrear, but there will be no complementary financial breakthrough to complement.

Every glory has a season of manifestation. The manifestation of one's glory does not stop that of the other. When one glory is at work to manifest, everything will cooperate with the breakthrough and success of the one. God put glory in his work so that men may see the wonders of His power in the work of His hand.

When a man's financial glory find expression to manifest, his life will be the center of financial fortune. Money will befriend his destiny. Everything he does will attract so much money that will make him very rich.

One beautiful thing about this glory is that everyman has their own measure of glory. Every man's glory is incomparable. It is important one's individual financial glory manifest, so that you can enjoy the beauty of your labor.

Scriptural declaration:
Thou shalt also decree a thing, and it shall be established unto thee: and the light shall shine upon thy ways. Job 22:28
He hath swallowed down riches, and he shall vomit them up again: God shall cast them out of his belly. Job 20:15

Prayers
1. Oh Lord, have mercy on me in Jesus name.
2. Oh Lord, hear my voice and empower my command in Jesus name.

3. You my financial glory, hear the voice of my command, manifest in the name of Jesus.

4. Doors of my financial glory, open by fire in the name of Jesus.

5. Every enemy of my financial glory, be located by the fire of the Holy Ghost and die in the name of Jesus.

6. Every covering and hindrance to my financial glory be remove completely in the name of Jesus.

28
Breaking Out Of The Prison Of Poverty

But this [is] a people robbed and spoiled; [they are] all of them snared in holes, and they are hid in prison houses: they are for a prey, and none delivereth; for a spoil, and none saith, Restore. Isa 42:22

Many people have been imprisoned by poverty. When a man is imprisoned, his glory, and what you can possibly become will also be imprisoned. Prison is not a place, because stars are not made in prison. Any one in prison is limited to what they can do and achieve. However, if anyone is locked up in the prison of poverty, it takes freedom from that prison to enter into their financial inheritance.

For out of prison he cometh to reign; whereas also [he that is] born in his kingdom becometh poor. Eccl 4:14

When a person is in the prison of poverty, his life cannot find expression. It is when he is out of that prison that is ideas and life can gain financial relevance. Prisoners are not save, they are victims of circumstances, until they find a relief and freedom.

The prison of poverty has kept many under the hold of poverty and their lives do not make any financial relevance. They are wretched, downtrodden, and frustrated. A prison cannot move far, he will only live in the confinement of whatever he has. If no one brings you anything, you will not enjoy anything except for the fact that God is with

Prison is not a place to be. To be imprisoned is to be limited, to be imprisoned is to be denied of the ability to pursue your dreams the way you want. To be imprisoned is to be denied the privilege to benefit from the common wealth of the nation. No organization can make a prison an ambassador, or appoint a prison in a major office, except inside the prison. No one can celebrate a prisoner or celebrate the achievement of the prison in the prisoner. The same thing applies to anyone in the prison of poverty.

No prison can break out of prison on his own, because the prison authority will not permit him. What made the job of the prison director, warders and executives active and considerable is the fact that they have prisoners in their custody. Without a prisoner in their custody, they will be out of job. That is why not all prisoners in a particular prison can be released, except one or more at a time. And no prison is without a prisoner. Prisoners must always be in every prison. Any man in prison is not the only one in prison. His dream, his vision, his potential, his aspiration and ambition are all in prison. But when he comes out of prison, all that belongs to him physically and spiritually will also come out. And it takes God to take a man out of prison, because the captors don't want the captive to be free.

How art thou fallen from heaven, O Lucifer, son of the morning! [how] art thou cut down to the ground, which didst weaken the nations! [That] made the world as a wilderness, and destroyed the cities thereof; **[that] opened not the house of his prisoners?** *Isa 14:12, 17.*

The powers in charge of prisons don't want their prisoners to go free. It is their joy they have prisoners locked up in their prison. Many people have been locked up in the prison of Satan, and as a result they are held fast and unable to move. But as the Lord lives, you are coming out.

Way out of prison:

1. Accept Jesus.

    Jesus is the savior. He has the authority and ordercity to save a man from the prison of poverty. He became poor so that you can become rich. He has exchange your poverty for riches, 2Cor. 8;9, just as he has exchanged your death for his life. Rom. 6:23.

2. Serve God: 1Sam. 2:7-8

    It is God that makes rich and makes poor. In His blessing lie riches. When the shower of blessing comes upon your life, it will drain the atmosphere of poverty and usher in flow of blessing.

3. Be prayerful. Luke 18:1-8

    Pray without ceasing, to break the yoke of poverty. Pray you way out of the prison of poverty. Prayer is a force of freedom. When you enter into the force of prayer, every obstacles holding you down will release you and you will become a free man.

4. Be a giver. Luke 8:36

    Giving is a platform of receiving. When you give, you will open doors for greater blessing. You have to give up what you have to get what you need. Giving is a principle that works on the basis of whatever you give is what you get. Give and it shall be given back to you...pressed down and shaking together would men give to your bosom. Giving destroy the yoke of lack. It takes giving to overcome lack, it takes deliberate and continuous giving to overcome financial and material scarcity. When you give enough, you will get more than enough.

5. Do something. Eccl. 9:10
    Find a business or work to do. These are the channels of blessing. When you are working, God will bless what you do. If God's wants to bless you, he must give you a work to do. Whatsoever your hand finds to do, do it with all your might…don't be idle.

Scriptural confession

Bring my soul out of prison, that I may praise thy name: the righteous shall compass me about; for thou shalt deal bountifully with me. Ps 142:7

Let the sighing of the prisoner come before thee; according to the greatness of thy power preserve thou those that are appointed to die; Ps 79:11

As for thee also, by the blood of thy covenant I have sent forth thy prisoners out of the pit wherein [is] no water. Zech 9:11

Our soul is escaped as a bird out of the snare of the fowlers: the snare is broken, and we are escaped. Ps 124:7

Prayers

1. Oh Lord, arise and intervene in my financial situation in Jesus name.
2. Every net of poverty that has captured me, release me and be consumed by fire in Jesus name.
3. Every cage of poverty where in I am locked in, break open and let me go in Jesus name.

4. Every prison of poverty where I am locked with my glory, open by fire and release me in the name of Jesus.

5. Every prison of poverty, gate of poverty caging me, I command you to open in the name of Jesus.

6. I am coming out of the stronghold of poverty in Jesus name.

7. Anything that is keeping me in the prison of poverty, release me and let me go in the name of Jesus.

8. I release myself and my financial fortune out of every prison in Jesus name.

29

Aborting Attacks
Against Your Source Of Income

He disappointeth the devices of the crafty, so that their hands cannot perform [their] enterprise. Job 5:12

Some people are victims of spiritual attacks against their finance. When the enemy is attacking your personal or business finance, that is a satanic strategy to turn you wretched. Your source of income is the work you do or business you are doing. Often time, you cannot make money without doing one thing or the other. God promises to pour is blessings upon the works of your hands. God does not bless an empty hand, he bless a duty-full hand and a giving hand.

So your hands must be busy with one business or the other. However, it is important to prosper in the works of your hands. It is when the works of your hand is prospering that it will attract financial fortune into your life. It takes money to make your dreams come through.

Understand that before men were formed, powers of darkness has been operating and wandering upon the surface of the earth. 1Pet. 1:8. When men was formed, they began their operation against the sons of men. John 10:10. The devil came to kill good things, destroy good vision, steal virtue, glory and meaningful tools of achievement. Thank God for giving us victory through Christ. So these powers are in operation, and they find easy channel through which to operate, and they possess men and operate through men. It is important that you know, so many powers of darkness are in operation this days. They want to frustrate good intention, kill good things and waste good people. This is the reason fervent prayer is needed to wage war against every forces of hell waging war against the channels of your blessings.

For we wrestle not against flesh and blood, but against principalities, against powers, against the rulers of the darkness of this world, against spiritual wickedness in high [places]. Wherefore take unto you the whole armour of God that ye may be able to withstand in the evil day, and having done all, to stand. Eph 6:12-13.

The forces wrestling with you are not visible, they are wicked spiritual forces, they are striving to get rid of your business and close down the business, close down your source of income. They operate in different ways and with deliberate intention to make progress impossible, but you must arise to challenge them and overturn their works through prayers.

Scriptural confession

I will overturn, overturn, overturn, it: and it shall be no [more], until he come whose right it is; and I will give it [him]. Ezek 21:27

Thus saith the LORD, thy redeemer, and he that formed thee from the womb, I [am] the LORD that maketh all [things]; that stretcheth forth the heavens alone; that spreadeth abroad the earth by myself; That frustrateth the tokens of the liars, and maketh diviners mad; that turneth wise [men] backward, and maketh their knowledge foolish. Isa 44:24

Behold, I give unto you power to tread on serpents and scorpions, and over all the power of the enemy: and nothing shall by any means hurt you. Luke 10:19

Prayers

1. Oh Lord, settle me in Jesus name.
2. Oh Lord, have mercy on me and my business in Jesus name.
3. Oh Lord, arise to deliver my work and business from the hand of the enemies in Jesus name.
4. Oh Lord, defend my business and work for your name sake in Jesus name.
5. Oh Lord, every harm that has been done against my business breakthrough, let it be destroyed in Jesus name.
6. Oh Lord my father, every power militating and fighting against my business and the work of my hand stop their evil operation and disgrace them woefully in Jesus name.
7. Every doors of attack that has been opened against my business and work, be closed in the name of Jesus.
8. Every power assigned against my business be arrested by the consuming fire of God in the mighty name of Jesus.
9. Every hindrance and blockage against my channels of income, be uprooted and removed in the mighty name of Jesus.
10. Heavens of blessing and breakthrough open for my business in the name of Jesus.
11. Every power assigned to waste and cause loses in my business and the work of my hand, I stop your operation and I command you to be arrested by the consuming fire of God in the name of Jesus.
12. Oh Lord, turn around my business in the name of Jesus.

13. Oh Lord, open back every channels of blessing the enemy has blocked against me and my business in the name of Jesus.

14. Every gift, money and they have given to exchange my business glory, be destroyed and reverse in operation in the name of Jesus.

15. Oh God, approve my business breakthrough and testimonies in Jesus name.

16. Thank you Lord, for answered prayers in the name of Jesus.

30
Sending Back The Arrows Of Poverty

For, lo, the wicked bend [their] bow, they make ready their arrow upon the string, that they may privily shoot at the upright in heart. Ps 11:2

Evil arrows of poverty are a wicked satanic weapon that is fired from the coven of darkness into the life of their victim. Every satanic weapon is commanded to perform certain operation, why arrow of poverty is peculiar in it operation is because it is sent on an errand of causing the victim to remain poor. As long as that arrow is in the life of the victim, the victim will be poor. The injunction has been programmed into the wicked arrow, and the arrow in the life of the victim will function like a virus released into a computer system.

This prayer is peculiar, I went to a church to minister some years ago, and the Spirit of the Lord ministered to my hearing, that I should lead the people in this prayer of arrow of poverty. He made me know that, that is the reason why someone there is experiencing poverty. That means with all opportunity and effort, the person will be in abject poverty. So poverty can be programmed into someone's life through wicked evil arrow, but as you pray it out, God will deliver you.

No weapon that is formed against thee shall prosper; and every tongue [that] shall rise against thee in judgment thou shalt condemn. This [is] the heritage of the servants of the LORD, and their righteousness [is] of me, saith the LORD. Isa 54:17

It is written that no weapon fashioned against you shall prospered. In order word, evil arrow can be fashioned specifically against someone. You reading this, this may be the issue in your life. if an arrow is fired, it will remained there like as an installation of darkness to deliver it assignment. You must command the arrow to backfire so that poverty can get out of your life. The devil is at work using different method to keep many in the bondage of poverty.

When you are addressing a prayer of evil arrow, it is a prayer you must pray with every strength in you. That arrow must be removed and backfire, while it operation too has to come to an end in Jesus name. be determined in this section of prayer, because the purpose of this book is to ensure that anything that wants to keep you poor has to be destroyed, so that when you launch out into any business or venture you can succeed in that business physically and financially. Financially prosperity helps a business to increasingly grow and prosper.

What is required to pray through?
1. Give your life to Jesus
2. Pray with spiritual understanding
3. Engage fasting in the prayer
4. Pray it morning, afternoon and night
5. Believe in the power of God to deliver

Scriptural confession
In righteousness shalt thou be established: thou shalt be far from oppression; for thou shalt not fear: and from terror; for it shall not come near thee. Behold, they shall surely gather together, [but] not by me: whosoever shall gather together against thee shall fall for thy sake. Behold, I have created the

smith that bloweth the coals in the fire, and that bringeth forth an instrument for his work; and I have created the waster to destroy. No weapon that is formed against thee shall prosper; and every tongue [that] shall rise against thee in judgment thou shalt condemn. This [is] the heritage of the servants of the LORD, and their righteousness [is] of me, saith the LORD.

As soon as they hear of me, they shall obey me: the strangers shall submit themselves unto me.
The strangers shall fade away, and be afraid out of their close places. Ps 18:44-45

Prayers

1. Oh Lord my father, have mercy on me today in the name of Jesus.
2. Oh Lord my father, hear me speedily in the name of Jesus.
3. Arrows of poverty fire into my life, come out by the authority in the name of Jesus.
4. Every evil arrows constituting poverty physically, spiritually and financially into my life come out by fire in the name of Jesus.
5. Powers behind evil arrows, here you judgment, receive fire and die by fire in the name of Jesus.
6. Powers behind operation of poverty in my life, be exposed and destroyed in the name of Jesus.
7. Every condition of poverty in my life, expire in the name of Jesus.
8. Every injunction of poverty in my life, be **reversed** in the name of Jesus.
9. Every program of poverty in my life, expire in the name of Jesus.

10. Ancient arrows and present arrows of poverty working together in my life and business expire and come out in the name of Jesus.

11. Holy Spirit, I invite you, deliver me by fire in the name of Jesus.

12. Thank you Jesus for answered prayers.

31

Deliverance From Spirit Spouse

This is one of the demonic spirits responsible for chronic poverty and frustration in life and marriage. The demonic powers behind some peoples cause of poverty is spirit spouse. It is a critical issue. Those who experience the operation of spirit spouse will understand this. It is not an issue that needed debate whether they are real or not. They are real.

Many people are experiencing wet dream because of the determinate operation of spirit spouse. This spirit spouse is the ancestral spirit that the victim has been dedicated to one way or the other.

It is one of the greatest mysteries in life. Though it should not be surprising, since we have the spirit world and the physical world. The spirit world is governed by strange and diverse spirits, and the real world is dominated by diverse kind of humans. But the operating of demons in the spirit world, extend to the physical world.

Spirit husband is called incubus, according to Oxford advance learner's dictionary, incubus is defined as a male evil spirit that has sex with a sleeping woman. This spirit engages in sexual activity with human being, not spirit being, while he is a spirit being.

The same goes with the spirit wife called, succubus, which specializes in having affairs with a real man. This spirit spouse is quiet different from a mermaid. This spirit spouse are married to their victim, or dedicated to their victim. And they will remain with their victim for as long as they refuse to separate themselves physically and spiritually from them.

They are fond of engaging their victims in all manner of romantic and sexual pervasion that will cause setback, pain and hardship for that spouse. While some, even take care of their human partners physically. And this spirit spouse can choose to appear physically to their victim, while some only appears in the dream. Nevertheless, the operation of this spirit spouse has to be terminated completely, for the victim to experience total freedom from their bondage and hardship.

Biblical origin of spirit spouse, The Living bible read as follows

Now a population explosion took place upon the earth. It was at this time that beings from the spirit world look upon the beautiful earth women and took them they desired to be their wives… in those days and even afterwards when the evil beings from the spirit world were sexually involved with human women, their children became giants, of who so many legends are told. Gen. 6: 1-4

Characteristics of spirit spouse
1. They are demonic in nature.
2. They terrorize their victim in the dream and physical
3. They are stubborn and notorious.
4. They are very jealous seeing the victim with another human partner.

5. They are serious with their assignment as if they are physically married to their victim.
6. They don't go easily; they want to remain permanently in the life of the victim.
7. They affect marriage of their victim, negatively.
8. They can kill their victim suddenly,
9. They make their victim engage in immoral sexual activities, like masturbation, pornography, etc.
10. They are responsible for hardship in their victim's marriage, and also causes divorces in that marriage.
11. They spirit spouse will terrify and torment the victim's real life partners.
12. They cause poverty, hardship and difficulties for their victim and even their spouse most times. Etc

There are different kinds of spirit spouse
1. Marine spirit spouse.
2. Ancestral spirit spouse.
3. Witchcraft spirit spouse.
4. Familiar spirit spouse.
5. Foundational spirit spouse etc.

How to be delivered from them
1. Accept Jesus into your life. John 8:32
2. Go for general or personal deliverance in a deliverance ministry. John 8:36
3. Invite Holy Spirit to join you in prayers. 2Cor. 3:17
4. Pray aggressively with the desire to be free. Ps. 34:17

Scriptural confession:
And the Lord shall deliver me from every evil work, and will preserve [me] unto his heavenly kingdom: to whom [be] glory forever and ever. Amen. 2Tim 4:18

Shall the prey be taken from the mighty, or the lawful captive delivered?
But thus saith the LORD, Even the captives of the mighty shall be taken away, and the prey of the terrible shall be delivered: for I will contend with him that contendeth with thee, and I will save thy children.
And I will feed them that oppress thee with their own flesh; and they shall be drunken with their own blood, as with sweet wine: and all flesh shall know that I the LORD [am] thy Saviour and thy Redeemer, the mighty One of Jacob. Isa 49:24-26.

Prayers
1. Holy Spirit, I invite you into my life to deliver me in Jesus name.
2. Mercy of God, speak for me in Jesus name.
3. Every evil covenant with any spirit spouse, break by the blood of Jesus.
4. Every ancestral evil altar engineering the manifestation of spirit spouse in my life, catch fire in the name of Jesus.
5. Any evil dedication that has been done for me to any spirit spouse be nullified by the blood of Jesus.
6. Every garment and property of spirit spouse in my life, catch fire in the name of Jesus.
7. Powers backing up the operation of spirit spouse in my life die in the name of Jesus.
8. Any spirit wife or husband in my life, release me and die in the name of Jesus.

9. Every ground that ancestral spirits has gained in my life, I recover it back in the name of Jesus.

10. Every evil link, covenant, dedication, agreement, vows, oaths, backing up the operation of spirit spouse in my life, be destroyed by the blood of Jesus.

11. Anything I am married to that is not of God, either knowingly or unknowingly, I renounce you today, be expose and destroyed in Jesus name.

12. Every altar of spirit spouse in my life and body, I command the fire of God to locate you in Jesus name.

13. Any initiation into spirit spouse bondage, be nullified and break in the name of Jesus.

14. Any spirit spouse or spirit children in my life, I reject you and renounce you totally in the mighty name of Jesus.

15. Holy Ghost fire, deliver me in the name of Jesus.

32
Overcoming the Spirit of Laziness

One of the major reasons of poverty is laziness. Laziness is an hindrance to success. Wealth does not flow to the doorstep of a lazy man. Riches is acquired by hard work. Anyone who cannot work hard towards becoming rich cannot work to sustain the riches. See what the scriptures say.

I went by the field of the slothful, and by the vineyard of the man void of understanding; And, lo, it was all grown over with thorns, [and] nettles had covered the face thereof, and the stone wall thereof was broken down. Then I saw, [and] considered [it] well: I looked upon [it, and] received instruction. [Yet] a little sleep, a little slumber, a little folding of the hands to sleep: So shall thy poverty come [as] one that travelleth; and thy want as an armed man. Prov. 24:30-34

Breaking through into financial rest is a product of diligence, after putting in prayer, you have to work towards your financial opportunities. When opportunities that will make you rich is at hand, it is your ability to work that will materialize the opportunity into prosperity. Laziness is an opportunity wasting habit in people who has it. You cannot afford to allow the spirit of laziness to keep you in the arena of poverty. Poverty is no man's inheritance, but it is a choice for anyone who wants to be poor to be. However, because you are poor now does not mean you are lazy, because you were born poor also does not mean you must remain poor. In every poor man is a rich man. Those who rose out of poverty into prosperity has seen the prosperity in them above the poverty they were born and so they break out of the shell and limitation of poverty into the atmosphere of prosperity.

Every excuse you can accommodate that will accommodate poverty has to be eradicated. Do everything to break the yoke of poverty in your life. if laziness is the yoke of poverty in your life, you must be willing to break the foothold of laziness in your life. don't let laziness kill the prosperity in you. Arise up above laziness and excuses and work at that opportunity with everything within you.

How To Overcome The Spirit Of Laziness

1. **Prayerfully overcome it**
   The reason you must prayerfully overcome is because, if it is the spirit of poverty, the spirit has to be bound, if it is the nature of laziness, the nature has to be broken through the force of prayer and the anointing of the Holy Spirit. Prayer is a force that brings transformation into one's life.

2. **Decide to overcome it**
   There is power in decision. The ability to take decision is the first key to release, and after the decision is taking the power to stand on your decision is another key to total freedom from the hold of laziness. Allow nothing to tamper with your decision. Decide and stand by it.

3. **Be discipline at your work**
   Be discipline. Discipline is the ability to keep to your routine whether you feel like it or not. The ability to be diligent when you don't feel like it is discipline. Discipline

will chain down the habit of laziness. After praying through, deciding to overcome and finally discipline.

Scriptures to confess

Verily I say unto you, Whatsoever ye shall bind on earth shall be bound in heaven: and whatsoever ye shall loose on earth shall be loosed in heaven. Matt 18:18

Wherefore God also hath highly exalted him, and given him a name which is above every name:
That at the name of Jesus every knee should bow, of [things] in heaven, and [things] in earth, and [things] under the earth; And [that] every tongue should confess that Jesus Christ [is] Lord, to the glory of God the Father. Phil 2:9

Prayers

1. Holy Spirit have your way in my life in the name of Jesus.
2. I lose myself from the spirit of laziness and slothfulness in the name of Jesus.
3. I bind every spirit of laziness in my life in the name of Jesus.
4. Every yoke of laziness in my life, break by fire in the name of Jesus.
5. Every hold of laziness over my life, release me by the authority in the name of Jesus.
6. Every curse of poverty, hereditary and gene of laziness in my life, break by the authority in the name of Jesus.
7. Power of God for diligence possesses me in the name of Jesus.
8. Anointing of the Holy Spirit lose me from laziness in the name of Jesus.

9. Every mindset of laziness in me, come out and fade away in the name of Jesus.

10. Every limitation laziness has brought into my life be removed by the authority in the mighty name of Jesus.

11. Oh Lord, give me another opportunity in the name of Jesus.

33
Releasing Your Prosperity In Captivity

He hath swallowed down riches, and he shall vomit them up again: God shall cast them out of his belly. Job 20:15

The devil came to kill, to steal and to destroy. One of the mission of the devil is to steal. Many people's prosperity has been stolen by the devil and has been kept in a demonic warehouse. As a result, this required some force to take back what the devil has stolen. According to that scripture, the enemy swallowed up riches, and he shall vomit them up again.

The riches that were stolen was that of Job. But when it vomited it, he was restored twice. To deliver your prosperity in captivity, you need to pray aggressively because the devil loves to steal and retain. Anything in his custody is hardly release. You can't plead for the devil to release it, you can only fight to possess it. See what Jesus said,

No man can enter into a strong man's house, and spoil his goods, except he will first bind the strong man; and then he will spoil his house. Mark 3:27

Every goods in the custody of a strong man is secure, until there is a higher power to subject the strongman and then take over the goods in his custody. The strongman in that picture represents the power of darkness in charge of other demons. You must be discerning and determine to overthrow the strongman and then subdue the strongman that has been in charge of your riches and family riches, there is all chances you are going to recover back if you can pray very well.

What you need to understand
1. Riches can be stolen spiritually and kept
2. Riches can be diverted
3. Riches can be hindered
4. Riches can be manipulated. That means what is supposed to come to you will be manipulated and given to another person. And that is a loose. You must know how to pray your way through and possess what is your.

Just as it is in the physical realm so it is in the spiritual realm, but the peculiar difference is that the spiritual controls the physical. Issues are first settled in the realm of the spirit before it manifest in the physical. You must change the effect of what you see in the spirit to what you desire in the physical.

To release your prosperity in captivity, you will need to engage in violent prayers.

Scriptural confession
And from the days of John the Baptist until now the kingdom of heaven suffereth violence, and the violent take it by force. Matt 11:12

He hath swallowed down riches, and he shall vomit them up again: God shall cast them out of his belly. Job 20:15

Prayers
1. Any where house of darkness, warehouse my riches, glory and virtue release them and catch-fire in Jesus name.

2. Every evil chain, chord, rope tying down my riches, and virtues break by fire in the name of Jesus.

3. Every evil cloth/garment that is used to cover my riches be removed and catch-fire in the name of Jesus.

4. Oh Lord my father, release your Angel that specializes in recovery now for my sake in the name of Jesus.

5. Angel of God that specializes in recovery of riches, glory and virtue go out and recover back my riches in the name of Jesus.

6. Every decree tying down my riches I break you in the name of Jesus, be reversed completely.

7. Any evil condition that is backing up the release of my riches be aborted now by the authority in the name of Jesus.

8. Every evil diversion channel in my life, I block it with the blood of Jesus in the name of Jesus. Amen.

9. My prosperity in captivity your time is up, be release by fire in the name of Jesus.

10. Power assigned to stop my prosperity, die by fire in the name of Jesus.

11. Powers hijacking my prosperity, you will not prosper, release it and die in Jesus name.

12. I command the release of all my physical and spiritual riches that has been denied me over the years in the name of Jesus Christ.

13. Oh Lord, arise and deliver into my hands my prosperity in Jesus name.

14. Thank you Lord Jesus for answering my prayers.

34

Victory Over Dream Criminals and Robbers

*When I say, My bed shall comfort me, my couch shall ease my complaint;
Then thou scarest me with dreams, and terrifiest me through visions:
So that my soul chooseth strangling, [and] death rather than my life. Job
7:13-15*

Dream criminals are the powers of darkness that operate against people's destiny through the vehicle of dream. Dream is an avenue to see into the future. Dream simply shows us the plans of God and also exposes the plans of the enemy. Dream is designed by God and not the devil. However, the devil uses the vehicle of dream to manipulate people's destiny into perpetual experience of failure.

Dream criminals are powers that have mastered the art of using dream to destroy the destiny of their victim and turning it to whatever they like. They rob their victim of good things through their dream and empty their lives in the physical. Since, the spiritual controls the physical. They have decided the shape and outcome of their daily lives through their evil dream operations.

Dream criminals can abort anything in their life of their victim through dream. As long as you are concern you must overcome dream criminal if you are going to make it. Dream criminal monitor good things coming into your life and harvest it before it manifest. They are the power that wastes the oncoming opportunity of their victims. Dream is so powerful that the destiny of a man can be turned upside down by the virtue of a negative dream. One negative dream can wreck havoc to a great destiny. In other word, dream can be used as satanic weapon to destroy the destiny of a person. Every weapon the devil is employing against your destiny must be exposed and destroyed through violent prayers.

Dreams robbers are powers that operate through the vehicle of dream to steal from their victim. They steal virtue, blessing, babies, glory and whatever is coming the way of their victim. Dream robbers monitor good things that are coming and boycott it to deny their victim of it. If you are victim of this spirits, you need to pray very well. If all that will do you good in life is stolen with nothing left for you, you cannot amount to what you want to. But through fervent prayers and determination you can stop the operation of dream robbers and criminals. Dream robbers are specialist in their field of operation in the life of their victim. They can steal what is coming the way of their victim, and can also steal what their victim has possessed already in the physical.

The operations of dream criminals and robbers
1. They kill good things at infancy
2. They steal and divert good things
3. They destroy good things.

How to be free from them
1. Discover their operations in your life.
2. Embarking on fasting
3. Pray violently against them.

Scriptural confession

He that committeth sin is of the devil; for the devil sinneth from the beginning. For this purpose the Son of God was manifested, that he might destroy the works of the devil. 1John 3:8

Be pleased, O LORD, to deliver me: O LORD, make haste to help me. Ps 40:13

Prayers

1. Blood of Jesus sanitize my dream life in the name of Jesus.
2. Power of God possesses my dream life in the name of Jesus.
3. Every dream criminal in charge of my life, I send you into exile forever in the name of Jesus.
4. Every mandate of dream criminal in life, expire in the name of Jesus.
5. Every operation of dream criminal in my life expire in the name of Jesus.
6. Every good thing dream criminal has stolen from me, I recover back in the name of Jesus.
7. Every good thing dream criminal has exchange in my life through dream, I command a total recovery in the name of Jesus.
8. Every evil deposit of dream criminal in my life be uprooted in the name of Jesus.
9. Every satanic agent of evil dream oppressing my life through dream, I command your death in the name of Jesus.
10. Every dream of demotion, hardship, problem in my life expire in the name of Jesus.

11. Every covenant of evil dream in my life, break in the name of Jesus.

12. I command the dream of prosperity and success into my life in the name of Jesus.

35
Breaking The Yoke of Financial Hardship

For it shall come to pass in that day, saith the LORD of hosts, [that] I will break his yoke from off thy neck, and will burst thy bonds, and strangers shall no more serve themselves of him: Jer. 30:8

The yoke of financial hardship is the yoke of poverty. Anything under a yoke is under bondage. Yoke is a satanic weapon that is employed in holding something captive. When an evil yoke is at work, it holds captive the blessing of the person in question that it is programmed against. Evil yoke of financial hardship causes abject poverty.

Yoke of financial hardship is a weapon of darkness, to make making money impossible no matter all the effort put in place to make the money. Infact, the more effort put in place the more the hardship. It is a yoke that will make a man to labor in vain financially. It will make a person to lose his financial opportunities and make money a perpetual scarce commodity in the life of the victim. It also ensures that all financial opportunity is wasted and all financial hope is dashed. There will be no relevant amount of money that will ever come into the hand of the victim. The victim will only survive on peanut.

If you are experiencing any of this financial hardship trait, it is important you embark on fasting with your prayers and pray with determination to be free forever in the name of Jesus. I can see God at work, willing to deliver you completely from all evil yokes and bring you into the harem of wealth.

Weapons For Destroying Yokes

1. Prayers:

And call upon me in the day of trouble: I will deliver thee, and thou shalt glorify me. Ps 50:15. Prayer is a weapon we have be given to do warfare and to command victory over every unwanted physical and spiritual situation in our lives. Every other weapon is activated by the word of your prayer.

2. Fasting:

[Is] not this the fast that I have chosen? to loose the bands of wickedness, to undo the heavy burdens, and to let the oppressed go free, and that ye break every yoke? Isa 58:6. You can go on 7days fast or 21 days from 6am to 6pm daily, to break every stubborn and ancestral yoke of poverty.

3. Anointing:

And it shall come to pass in that day, [that] his burden shall be taken away from off thy shoulder, and his yoke from off thy neck, and the yoke shall be destroyed because of the anointing. Isa 10:27. After your prayer and fasting, employ the use of the anointing oil. Pour the oil on your head and hands and command every yoke to lose you and break in Jesus name.

4. Authority in the name of Jesus:

All nations compassed me about: but in the name of the LORD will I destroy them. Ps 118:10. Jesus is our Lord, and there is power and authority in his name to destroy evil works and also deliver his own people. His name does not expire, neither is it ever powerless.

5. **The Word of God:**

   He sent his word, and healed them, and delivered [them] from their destructions. Ps 107:20

   The word of God is a living word that has the power to deliver and transform any life and situation if it is applied in faith.

Scriptural confessions:

For now will I break his yoke from off thee, and will burst thy bonds in sunder. Nah. 1:13.

Prayers

1. Oh Lord, you are the yoke breaker; break every yokes in my life in Jesus name.
2. Every yoke of financial hardship in my life, break in the mighty name of Jesus.
3. The anointing to break every evil yoke, oh Lord, release upon me in Jesus name.
4. Blood of Jesus, locate every yoke in mu life and destroy it in Jesus name.
5. Every power of evil yoke of financial hardship be destroyed in Jesus name.
6. Every ancestral yoke of poverty and hardship break in the name of Jesus.
7. Every yoke of financial bondage in my life break by fire in the name of Jesus.
8. Every evil yoke making it impossible for me to break through, break in the name of Jesus.

36

Setting The Garment Of Poverty Ablaze

Then Jacob said unto his household, and to all that [were] with him, Put away the strange gods that [are] among you, and be clean, and change your garments: Gen 35:2

There are different kinds of spiritual garments. Every garment has it uniqueness and peculiar impact in the life of the wearer. When it comes to the operation of the work of darkness, it is a mystery. As dark powers will do everything possible and take every devise possible to achieve the mission in the life of their victim. The garment of poverty is a spiritual garment that is meant to function as an instrument of poverty in the life of her victim, thereby ensuring that the victim leave in abject poverty, all her life.

The kind of garment your spirit man is wearing in the realm of the spirit determines the kind of physical experience you have in real life. Your spiritual garments determine what you attract. If you are putting on a garment of royalty, it will make you receive honor from men. If you put on the garment of shame, it will make one's experience to be that of shame. If it is a garment of prosperity, prosperity will naturally find it way to you.

Your garment determines your color and your garment also determines the way people approach you to honor you. The way your physical garment determines your physical reception, your spiritual garment determines your reception.

Garment of poverty upon any man will keep the person in the bondage of deep poverty. A spiritual garment symbolizes that the operation of the enemy is in the life of the victim and the person will be in the prison of poverty. However If you have been feeling the presence of a strange garment upon you, it is time to pray it out of your life. Garment of poverty will make the victim a candidate of poverty. If you don't want to be a garment of poverty, you must pray out of your life anything that can attract poverty spiritually into your life. Poverty is the enemy of vision. A poor man will struggle to actualize his dream, especially if he has any of this spiritual element of poverty that wants to keep him in poverty.

How To Overcome Evil Garments
1. Accept Jesus.
2. Engage the fire of the Holy ghost
3. Pray violently
4. Pray till you have inner conviction that it has been settled

Scriptural confession
And he will destroy in this mountain the face of the covering cast over all people, and the vail that is spread over all nations. Isa 25:7

But he answered and said, Every plant, which my heavenly Father hath not planted, shall be rooted up. Matt 15:13

Prayers
1. Oh Lord, have mercy on me in Jesus name.
2. Oh Lord, arise to my deliverance in Jesus name.
3. Oh Lord, send down your fire for my deliverance in the name of Jesus.

4. Angel of deliverance appear and deliver me in the name of Jesus.

5. Every garment of poverty in my life be removed by fire and catch fire in Jesus name.

6. Every evil garment that constitutes poverty in my life, be roosted by fire in Jesus name.

7. Blood of Jesus set me free in Jesus name.

8. Every ancestral evil garment upon me your time is up, I put you off in the name of Jesus.

9. Any power assigned to keep me in poverty, your appointment is terminated in the name of Jesus.

10. Anything assigned to keep me in poverty, release me and dies in the name of Jesus.

11. Anointing of poverty in my life, dry up in the name of Jesus.

12. Anointing of favor rest upon me in Jesus name.

13. Anointing of prosperity, fall upon me in the name of Jesus.

14. Garment of glory from the almighty come upon me in the name of Jesus.

15. Garment of prosperity come upon me in the name of Jesus.

37

Beheading The Serpent Of Poverty

In that day the LORD with his sore and great and strong sword shall punish leviathan the piercing serpent, even leviathan that crooked serpent; and he shall slay the dragon that [is] in the sea. Isa 27:1

Serpent in this case is a demonic spirit that is worshipped in many families. This kind of spirit has been operating in those families for years and their forefathers has referenced and worshipped this serpent. As far as they are concerned, that serpent is their god. They look up to the serpent as their savior, thou not one. But for those who have cut away from worshipping this god of their fathers, has been under the affliction of poverty by the operation of this evil family serpent. That is why in such family it is abominable to kill serpent, it is abominable to eat serpent, it is abominable

Many families that are victim of serpentine frustration and operation are under perpetual bondage and difficulties. As long as you allow this serpent to dictate the affairs of your life, all the virtues of blessings that can make your life worthwhile will be captured and kept under the belly of this serpent. Any serpent that is in operation to swallow prosperity in your family shall be beheaded in Jesus name.

Other operation of this serpent
1. They are behind poverty
2. They are behind lust
3. They are behind confusion
4. They causes frustration and acute difficulty

5. They are behind affliction
6. They cause strange movement in the body
7. They cause fear

How to overcome
1. Give your life to Jesus.
2. Pray to destroy it.

Scriptural confession
In that day the LORD with his sore and great and strong sword shall punish leviathan the piercing serpent, even leviathan that crooked serpent; and he shall slay the dragon that [is] in the sea. Isa 27:1

He hath swallowed down riches, and he shall vomit them up again: God shall cast them out of his belly. Job 20:15

That which he laboured for shall he restore, and shall not swallow [it] down: according to [his] substance [shall] the restitution [be], and he shall not rejoice [therein]. Job 20:18

Prayers
1. Oh Lord, release unto me your sword of fire in Jesus name.
2. I dissociate myself from every ancestral serpent, family serpent, evil serpent in the name of Jesus.
3. Any serpent residing in my body, come out and die in the name of Jesus.
4. Any serpentine power operating in my life die in the name of Jesus.

5. Every serpentine spirit assigned against my life and prosperity, be arrested by the fires of the Holy Ghost in the name of Jesus.

6. Every serpentine bondage in my life, break by fire in the name of Jesus.

7. Any serpentine covenant in my life break by fire in the name of Jesus.

8. Every serpentine yoke in my like break by fire in the name of Jesus.

9. Every serpentine mark and symbol in my body be removed by the blood of Jesus in the name of Jesus.

10. Every altar of serpent in my family, collapses and catch fire in the name of Jesus.

11. Every serpent of poverty, die in the name of Jesus.

12. Every serpent swallowing up virtues, glory and blessing in my life and family, be vomit all the good things you have swallowed up and be consumed by the fire of the Holy Ghost in the name of Jesus.

13. Oh Lord my father, behead every serpent in my life and family in Jesus name.

14. Every serpent of affliction, expire and die in the name of Jesus.

15. Every serpent of lust, come out and die in the name of Jesus.

16. Blood of Jesus, set me free from every serpent in the name of Jesus.

17. Holy Ghost fire, locate every serpent in my life and consume them in the name of Jesus.

18. Every monitoring and flying serpent assigned against my life, wherever you may be I command the fire of God to locate you now, and be destroyed in the name of Jesus.

19. I separate myself from every evil serpent in the name of
Jesus.

20. All that has been captured through this serpent, I
command the release in the name of Jesus.

21. I command, let the Spirit of God take over every
operation of my life in the name of Jesus.

38

Breaking Down Every Evil Wall Of Resistance

Now Jericho was straitly shut up because of the children of Israel: none went out, and none came in.
And the LORD said unto Joshua, See, I have given into thine hand Jericho, and the king thereof, [and] the mighty men of valour.
And ye shall compass the city, all [ye] men of war, [and] go round about the city once. Thus shalt thou do six days.
And seven priests shall bear before the ark seven trumpets of rams' horns: and the seventh day ye shall compass the city seven times, and the priests shall blow with the trumpets.
And it shall come to pass, that when they make a long [blast] with the ram's horn, [and] when ye hear the sound of the trumpet, all the people shall shout with a great shout; and the wall of the city shall fall down flat, and the people shall ascend up every man straight before him.
And Joshua the son of Nun called the priests, and said unto them, Take up the ark of the covenant, and let seven priests bear seven trumpets of rams' horns before the ark of the LORD. Josh. 6:1-6

As the name suggest, wall of resistance is a spiritual wall and barricade around a person and there breakthrough, this wall serve as a difficult hindrance in breaking into one's desired haven. Every wall of resistance serves as a barrier against the next phase, next chapter and next level of one's life, business and expectation. any obstacles is not permitted to be tolerated in any capacity. Every resistance has to be addressed as an enemy. If a wall of resistance is built around a man, life will be so difficult that to succeed will be difficult. This wall has to be addressed and pulled down by the authority in the name of Jesus.

God said, he has given the children of Israel the land of Jericho as theirs; however the wall of the city was so strong that it could not be pulled down by the men of war, but it took the involvement of the God of war to pull down the wall. If the wall of Jericho was not pulled down, the promise of God would not come to pass. Every wall of Jericho in your life has to be pulled down if you are to enter into your next phase of success.

In this book no prayer topic is the same, and the truth is that every prayer topic will bring deliverance to many people in bondage of financial hardship that the source has remain untraceable.

Many people are not poor because they were born poor, but the powers that kept their parent in poverty want to continue operation in their lives. And some however, was born rich, but some forces brought down into the circle of the poor. In any category you find yourself, you have to pray very wall.

Wall of resistance will frustrate all effort and ability put in place to breakthrough. It is until this wall is broken down that you can actually experience surprising financial and business turn around.

Scriptural confession
Casting down imaginations, and every high thing that exalteth itself against the knowledge of God, and bringing into captivity every thought to the obedience of Christ; 2Cor 10:5

For verily I say unto you, That whosoever shall say unto this mountain, Be thou removed, and be thou cast into the sea; and shall not doubt in his heart, but shall believe that those things which he saith shall come to pass; he shall have whatsoever he saith. Mark 11:23

Prayers
1. Oh Lord my father, I invite you to help me overcome this great obstacle in the name of Jesus.
2. Every mountain of difficulty and poverty before me, melt by the fire of God in the name of Jesus.
3. Oh Lord my father, the way you pull down the wall of Jericho pull down every wall of resistance in my life in the name of Jesus.
4. Every wall of poverty, collapse by fire in the name of Jesus.
5. Every wall of resistance against my breakthrough, collapse in the name of Jesus.
6. Oh Lord my father, release your voice every wall of resistance in my life in the name of Jesus.
7. Every ancestral wall of resistance collapse in the name of Jesus.
8. Anything built around me and against my prosperity like a wall, hear the word of the Lord, collapse in Jesus name.

39

Commanding The Atmosphere of Prosperity

Hast thou commanded the morning since thy days; [and] caused the dayspring to know his place; Job 38:12

God has empowered every believer with the instruction and mandate to take charge of their life and command the result they want to see around them. Since you are in charge of all that God has made, He has given you divine order to command your morning, command your days, command your atmosphere, and command everything around you by the power in the name of Jesus.

God will never fill in the gap for you. He wants you to take charge and put to practice what He has instructed as a sign of faith in His word. You are in charge of the atmosphere around you. You determine a lot about what happens around you.

The atmosphere around you determines what comes into your sphere. There is a circle around you that is formed by the atmosphere. If you have grace filled atmosphere, you will experience the work of grace any where you find yourself. The spiritual atmosphere around you determines what you attract.

Atmosphere of prosperity is an atmosphere that attracts and welcomes prosperity. The right atmosphere, has the right spirit operating under that atmosphere, a negative atmosphere has opposing forces working in such atmosphere. So your atmosphere determines your utmost-phere. It determines how high you go, how well you grow, and how secured you are. Your atmosphere in order word determines what happens in your world, because your atmosphere is your world. Everyone has their own peculiar atmosphere that cannot be intercepted by any one. Everywhere you go, you carry your atmosphere with you.

You can create your own atmosphere by realizing the need to. Every atmosphere around is created consciously or unconsciously by you. The atmosphere filled with God's glory will attract goodness and mercy. You are the lord of your atmosphere, look deep into your present atmosphere, if it is not what you want, picture the atmosphere you want around you. Be it peace, love, favor etc. in the atmosphere of prosperity, the angels at work are the angel of blessing. They attract blessings into the life of the man with such atmosphere.

What Your Atmosphere Determines

- Your atmosphere determines the spirit around you.
- Your atmosphere determines your favor with people.
- Your atmosphere determines your success in what you do.
- Your atmosphere determines your far well.
- Your atmosphere is the subtotal of what gravitate towards you.
- Your atmosphere determines the doors that open unto you.
- Your atmosphere determines the level of your comfort. You cannot be comfortable in an unfriendly atmosphere. Create your atmosphere by commanding it by authority in Jesus name.

This atmosphere of prosperity is a spiritual atmosphere, though you can feel the unique presence of the atmosphere.

Kinds of atmosphere
1. Good atmosphere
2. Bad atmosphere
3. Divine atmosphere

Negative atmosphere
1. Atmosphere of rejection
2. Atmosphere of loses
3. Atmosphere of non achievement etc.

How To Transform Your Atmosphere

1. Prayerfully discover the common daily experience around your life.
2. If it is negative, then embark on serious prayer to end it.
3. If it is positive, pray to manifest greater glory.
4. Command the angels of God to surround you and fill your atmosphere with your heart desire according to the will of God.

Scriptural confession:
But the path of the just [is] as the shining light, that shineth more and more unto the perfect day. Prov 4:18

For thou wilt light my candle: the LORD my God will enlighten my darkness. Ps 18:28

They looked unto him, and were lightened: and their faces were not ashamed. Ps 34:5

Thou preparest a table before me in the presence of mine enemies: thou anointest my head with oil; my cup runneth over. Ps 23:5
Surely goodness and mercy shall follow me all the days of my life: and I will dwell in the house of the LORD forever. Ps 23:6
Wherefore he saith, Awake thou that sleepest, and arise from the dead, and Christ shall give thee light. Eph 5:14
And have no fellowship with the unfruitful works of darkness, but rather reprove [them]. Eph 5:11

Prayers

1. Oh Lord, empower me with your power of authority in Jesus name.
2. I command the fire of God to discharge every stranger in my atmosphere in Jesus name.
3. I break the hold of every strongman over and around my life in the name of Jesus.
4. I command the atmosphere around me to turn around to the atmosphere of blessing in Jesus name.
5. I break the grip of negative atmosphere around my life in Jesus name.
6. I decree that every curse, spell, evil word that has been released into the arena of my life, be broken in the name of Jesus.
7. I surround myself with the atmosphere of peace, favor, prosperity in the name of Jesus.
8. I command the angel of peace and prosperity into my life the name of Jesus.
9. Every negative atmosphere and circumstance around my life, be terminated and reverse to a good one in the name of Jesus.
10. I cover myself with the blood of Jesus.

40

Breaking The Curses Of Slavery

Being a slave is not an accident, slavery is a product of curse. Slaves are born like every other men are born. Only that every slave is programmed to serve others. Anyone under this curse, there destiny is connected to slavery. As some slavery is as a result of curse issued against that family, some are by birth. When the curse of slavery is upon a family or person, he will serve as slave and will not amount to anything. The best he can be is to be a chief slave. Slaves don't become kings of free men.

The Gibeonite were afraid of the children of Joshua and his men, and so they disguise like someone coming from a very distance country and came to the Israelite and enter alliance with them not to destroy them. few days later, the Israelite discovered that they were just neighbors and so they placed a curse upon the Gibeonites.

And Joshua called for them, and he spake unto them, saying, Wherefore have ye beguiled us, saying, We [are] very far from you; when ye dwell among us? Now therefore ye [are] cursed, and there shall none of you be freed from being bondmen, and hewers of wood and drawers of water for the house of my God. And they answered Joshua, and said, Because it was certainly told thy servants, how that the LORD thy God commanded his servant Moses to give you all the land, and to destroy all the inhabitants of the land from before you, therefore we were sore afraid of our lives because of you, and have done this thing. Josh 9:22-24

This is a critical area most men did not observe what is happening in their lives. Some men are not just born to serve others, but by the virtue of this kind of curse upon their destiny. They ended up serving others and leaving below their means.

If a person is placed under this kind of curse, all the money that will come into his hand is just for survival. He cannot handle money that can move his status to the level of nobles.

Destinies are crafted by words. The words program into your destiny determines the part it follows. And the effort you make to keep your destiny on the track of your vision also determines where you end. So everything is a choice of the person involved. You make the greatest choice of the outcome of your destiny. If they have used any curse or negative words to subject you to a state of slavery, you must stand up against it and make every spirit effort possible to reverse every havoc that has been done by the authority in Jesus name. Curse rewrite a man's destiny and determines a man's going in life.

If you want to breakthrough, you must break every hold of the curse of slavery upon you and your bloodline forever.

How to break this curse
1. Confirm if you are a victim
2. Give your life to Christ
3. Pray an effectual fervent prayer

Scriptural confession
Draw nigh unto my soul, [and] redeem it: deliver me because of mine enemies. Ps 69:18

Christ hath redeemed us from the curse of the law, being made a curse for us: for it is written, Cursed [is] every one that hangeth on a tree: Gal 3:13

Prayers
1. Oh Lord, have mercy upon me in Jesus name.
2. Every curse of slavery in my life be cancelled by the blood of Jesus
3. I break every yoke of slavery in my life in the name of Jesus
4. Every inherited family pattern of slavery in my life be destroyed by the blood of Jesus
5. Every spirit of slavery in my life I bind you in the name of Jesus.
6. Every element of slavery in my life, be destroyed in Jesus name.

41

Breaking Free From Witchcraft Operation

Witchcraft is a serious satanic act to pervert, bend, and distort situations to conform to their wicked plans. Witchcraft is an evil association and congregation of darkness, where evil plans are conjured against the destiny of mankind. Witchcraft spirit possess their victim and controls their will and act against God's will. The activities of witchcraft operation have been so pronounced and terrific. Many people suffers hardship as a result of the oppression of witchcraft.

And I will cut off witchcrafts out of thine land; and thou shalt have no more sooth sayers. Micah 5:12

Thou shalt not suffer a witch to live. Exod. 22:18

Witchcraft is a combination of witch and crafts. A witch is a person who manipulates things and people. He controls them to her own selfish and evil ambition. It is a person who casts spells, who recite incantation, involves in evil association whose aim is to destroy the destiny of man. She is a merciless spirit.

The crafts is their devices and weapons they use, with the skill they employed in using it to keep people under their bondage, oppression and suffering. E.g caging people physically or spiritually. Projecting evil attacks, and oppression. Promoting worldliness, pornography etc. killing, stealing and destroying man and his treasure. It takes God to deliver a person from these powers. Many families have atleast, one or more witchcraft agent in his or her family.

These powers can waste people's time, resources and opportunities. They can make life unbearable for their victim. They monitor their victim on a daily basis, to ensure that he does not amount to what God want him to.

Signs of witchcraft operation:
1. Financial problem and hardship.
2. Cobwebs, blockages and attacks
3. Hearing strange voices
4. Pocket leakage and debts
5. Eating in the dreams
6. Having wets dreams
7. Still birth and infancy death
8. Unexplainable delay, hatred and failure
9. Barrenness
10. Attack of insanity and strokes
11. They perpetuate, tragedy, accidents, plane crash, domestic accident etc.
12. Deformity
13. Acute frustration and depression
14. Family crises and storms
15. Attacks and bad dreams experience
16. Hindrances and disappointment in getting jobs, visa, marriage etcs.

How to overcome this acts
1. Giving your life to Jesus
2. Genuine repentance

3. Embark on 7days or more fasting and vigils
4. Pray violently against their activities you observe in your life
5. Don't be afraid and have faith in God.

Prayers
1. Every witchcraft operations in my life be exposed and destroyed in the name of Jesus
2. Every witchcraft agents attacking my life, release me and die in Jesus name.
3. Any witchcraft arrow in my spirit, soul and body, come out in the name of Jesus.
4. All witchcraft weapons fashioned against me, be roasted by the fire of the Holy Spirit in Jesus name.
5. Every witchcraft means of transportation, burn by fire in the name of Jesus.
6. Every stronghold of witchcraft against my life, collapses by fire in the name of Jesus.
7. Every witchcraft obstacles, hindrances and road block to breakthrough, be removed in the name of Jesus.
8. Every witchcraft agents in charge of my case, be exposed and die in the mighty name of Jesus.
9. Every witchcraft altars controlling and manipulating my life, fire of God, locate them and consume them in the name of Jesus.
10. All witchcraft plantations in my life, be uprooted by fire in the name of Jesus.
11. Every witchcraft projection against me be aborted by fire in the name of Jesus.
12. Every witchcraft agent holding on to the key of my breakthrough and prosperity, release them and die in the name of Jesus.

13. Oh Lord, deliver me from every witchcrafts activities and bondage in the name of Jesus.

14. Any witchcraft hand oppressing me and holding what belongs to me, I command you to wither by fire in the name of Jesus.

15. Every witchcraft covenant operating in my foundation and working against my life, break by fire in the name of Jesus.

16. Every legal ground of witchcraft in my life, be exposed and destroyed in the name of Jesus.

17. Every witchcraft embargo upon my business, life be lifted by fire in the name of Jesus

18. Oh Lord, arise and fight for me in the name of Jesus.

19. All that witchcraft agents has taken from me, I collect it back in the name of Jesus.

20. I break myself free from every hold of witchcraft in the mighty name of Jesus.

42
Wind of money, blow into my life

And there went forth a wind from the LORD, and brought quails from the sea, and let [them] fall by the camp, as it were a day's journey on this side, and as it were a day's journey on the other side, round about the camp, and as it were two cubits [high] upon the face of the earth. Num 11:31

See, there is a divine wind. When divine wind is at work, it works in your favor. Divine wind is the wind that comes from the Lord and it is employed in drawing your blessing that is in distance place. That scripture gives us account of a wind from the Lord that is a divine wind. Divine wind is more powerful than natural wind. Natural wind works in command of the weather. Natural wind will blow good things away, it will pull off house roofs, blow sand into people's eyes, and it can cause havoc. But divine wind will blow favor, will blow blessing, it will blow helpers, it would even blow money.

Wind of money is a divine wind that is commissioned to blow money. The way the wind of the Lord blew quails into the camp of the Israelite in so much that they cannot finish the quails. Divine wind will blow in money in so much that you cannot finish spending it.

Divine wind is one of the spiritual weapon God uses in actualizing his works of signs and wonder. Divine wind is the same wind that will blow in money into your life.

He sendeth out his word, and melteth them: he causeth his wind to blow, [and] the waters flow. Ps 147:18

God has a wind…the wind of God is powerful. It can blow whatever you command it to blow into your life. The wind cannot only blow things into your life, it can blow out what you don't want. The wind can blow off your adversary and their evil works.

And the LORD shall utterly destroy the tongue of the Egyptian sea; **and with his mighty wind** *shall he shake his hand over the river, and shall smite it in the seven streams, and make [men] go over dryshod. Isa 11:15*

The wind of the Lord is powerful. Wind blows things away from you or towards you. Use the wind in your favor. The wind of the Lord can blow in money. Sometimes ago I was in need of some money for some important things and the Lord told me, if the wind of money does not blow, money cannot come. Then I immediately commanded the wind of money to blow and money never ceased blowing in. There is a wind of money. It has to blow in money you need to actualize your dreams and vision. Command the wind of money to blow money into your business and your life now.

Types of wind
1. **Divine wind: Number 11:31**

    Divine wind is the wind we are engaging. It is a wind that comes from the Lord. It does not bring destruction to the people of God. It is one of the weapons of harvest of good things. It is used in recovering what has been lost or bringing to you what is meant for you but is so far away from you. The wind of the LORD is so weighty that no matter the size of the package of blessing, it can bring it.

2. **Evil wind: Job 1:19**

   Evil wind is a wind from the devil. It is a destructive wind that destroy every good things in it way. If an evil wind blows against a person, it will result to spiritual attack against the health of the person. And if it blows against people's finance, it will blow away the finance and leave the victim stranded.

Scriptures:

And there went forth a wind from the LORD, and brought quails from the sea, and let [them] fall by the camp, as it were a day's journey on this side, and as it were a day's journey on the other side, round about the camp, and as it were two cubits [high] upon the face of the earth. Num 11:31

Thou shalt also decree a thing, and it shall be established unto thee: and the light shall shine upon thy ways. Job 22:28

Prayers

1. Wind of money blow money into my life in the name of Jesus.
2. Oh Lord, connect me to my prosperity in Jesus name.
3. Wind of the Lord, blow away every obstacles and hindrance around my life in the name of Jesus.
4. Wind of the Lord, blow away every satanic cloud blocking flow of money in Jesus name.
5. Wind of the Lord, blow away every challenges causing setback in the name of Jesus.
6. Gate of wealth open unto me in the name of Jesus.
7. Window of blessing open to me in the name of Jesus.
8. Wind of money blow all around the world and blow my money into my hand in the name of Jesus.

43

Personal Deliverance Prayers

*And the Lord shall deliver me from every evil work, and will preserve [me]
unto his heavenly kingdom: to whom [be] glory forever and ever. Amen.
2Tim 4:18*

Personal deliverance prayers are prayers intended for your freedom. Freedom comes through deliverance. Violent freedom comes through violent prayer. There is necessity for personal deliverance if the cause of poverty is not among the prayers enlisted above. There are some personal problems that needed to be sorted first before financial fortune can be realized. Personal deliverance is needed for total liberation in all areas of a man's life. There is a need for personal deliverance if nothing is working in your life.

What is deliverance?

Deliverance means to be free from bondage of the enemy. Deliverance means to be set free from every satanic imprisonment. Deliverance to be loosed from evil chains, evil soul ties, evil covenant that is keep you bound to your adversary and problem. Deliverance means to liberate a man from all his problems and challenges. Deliverance means to know the truth and to act on the truth you know for you freedom.

He delivered me from my strong enemy, and from them which hated me: for they were too strong for me. Ps 18:17

Deliverance is when God himself comes to rescue you from that challenge, that problem, that stubborn adversary that has held you tight and vow not to lose his grip on you.

Who needs personal deliverance?

1. If you are frustrated in life.
2. If nothing is working in your hands, both business and other thing you do.
3. If you are experiencing difficulties and hardship.
4. If you are being challenged by demonic powers or strange demonic spirit.
5. If you are going through unexplainable problems that is not allowing you to breakthrough in life.

Keys for deliverance?

1. Willingness to be delivered
2. Unshakeable faith.
3. Violent prayers.
4. Lay hold on the truth. John 8:32

Scriptural confession:

Hear me speedily, O LORD: my spirit faileth: hide not thy face from me, lest I be like unto them that go down into the pit. Ps 143:7

Deliver me, O LORD, from mine enemies: I flee unto thee to hide me. Ps 143:9

Deliver me, O LORD, from the evil man: preserve me from the violent man; Which imagine mischiefs in [their] heart; continually are they gathered together [for] war. They have sharpened their tongues like a serpent; adders' poison [is] under their lips. Keep me, O LORD, from the hands of the wicked; preserve me from the violent man; who have purposed to overthrow my goings. The proud have hid a snare for me, and cords; they have spread a net by the wayside; they have set gins for me. I said unto the LORD, Thou [art] my God: hear the voice of my supplications, O LORD. Ps 140:1-6

And have no fellowship with the unfruitful works of darkness, but rather reprove [them]. Eph 5:11

Read the following bible verse in the anointing oil and use it. Romans 16:20, Luke 10:19, 2Tim. 4:18, Isaiah 10:27, Isaiah 14:1-3, Rev. 12:11, Ps. 27, John 14:13-14.

Prayers

1. Ask God to show you mercy in Jesus name.
2. In the name of Jesus I renounce every work of darkness in the name of Jesus.
3. I renounce and break every evil covenant in my life in Jesus name.
4. I break every soul tie between me and any personality in the name of Jesus.
5. I remove and uproot of evil plantation of the enemy that is making me victim of the enemy in Jesus name.
6. Every legal ground of the enemy against me, be destroyed in the name of Jesus.
7. Every battle through dream be destroyed in the name of Jesus.

8. Every evil plantation of the enemy in me, be uprooted by the mighty hand of God in Jesus name.

9. Every satanic imprisonment in my life, break lose in the name of Jesus.

10. Every ancestral captivity in my life, break lose in the name of Jesus.

11. Every satanic yoke operating in my life, break in the name of Jesus.

12. Every strongman assigned against my life, release me and die in Jesus name.

13. Blood of Jesus, set me from every bondage in Jesus name.

14. Every operation of darkness going on in my life, be aborted in Jesus name.

15. Every demonic spirit, strongman residing inside of me, come out in the name of Jesus and die.

16. Every satanic restriction upon my life and finance, be lifted in the name of Jesus.

17. Every embargo upon my finance and destiny be lifted in the name of Jesus.

18. I plead the blood of Jesus inside of me in Jesus name.

19. Oh Lord, command deliverance for me in the name of Jesus.

Conclusion

God has prepared to prosper you, but there are forces that are at work to stop you. Riches is not meant for some kind of fortunate people, but for anyone who desire it for the purpose of helping humanity. However this book is written to help you solve every challenge that can stop you from overcoming financial hardship and release you into financial ocean. Engage these resources with spiritual understanding and give it to others to use. This may be the treasure of wealth someone's destiny has been waiting for.

OTHER BOOKS BY THE AUTHOR

1. The Force Of Prayer

2. Business Breakthrough Prayers

3. Breaking The Yoke Of Financial Hardship

4. Secret Of Total Deliverance

5. Command Your Healing

6. Jackpot To Destiny Fulfilment